Bass Bug Fishing

Books by William G. Tapply

Bass Bug Fishing

William G. Tapply

The Lyons Press

First Edition

A condensed version of Chapter 1, "The Bass-Bug Moment," appeared in the January 1999 issue of *Gray's Sporting Journal.*

Material from Chapter 2, in expanded and significantly altered form, appeared in three parts in the "Roots" column of *Warmwater Fly Fishing* in 1999.

Printed in the United States of America

10 9 8 7 6 5 4 3 2 1

Library of Congress Cataloging-in-Publication Data
Tapply, William G.
    Bass bug fishing / William G. Tapply.
        p.   cm.
    Includes bibliographical references (p. 137) and index.
    ISBN 1-55821-789-4
    1. Bass fishing. 2. Bug fishing. 3. Bugs (Fishing lures)
I. Title.
SH681.T345 1999
799.1′773—dc21   99-17971
                                              CIP

For

H. G. "TAP" TAPPLY,
my father, editor, teacher, and lifetime partner,
and the inventor of the only bass bug
anyone will ever need.

Contents

Acknowledgments

The following people have contributed to this project, and to them all I am grateful:

Will Ryan shared his expertise, his wit, his books, and his boat with me;

John Likakis, the estimable editor of *Warmwater Fly Fishing*, helped me out with bugs and ideas and has given me space in his magazine to share mine;

Art Scheck, editor and wordsmith without peer, offered eye-opening wisdom on hard-bodied bugs;

Andy "Mr. Bass" Gill, master angler and my partner in frivolous pursuits, has shared many bassy moments with me;

Matthew Hodgson, collector of bass bugs and bass-bug lore, generously shared his memories, his stories, and his wisdom with me;

Nick Lyons encouraged me to do this book, and I hope to field-test all the theories in it with him;

Vicki Stiefel, my love, is an expert bluegill angler, and is becoming a bassmaster in her own right;

And I thank all the authors living and gone, whose bass-fishing writings informed and entertained me throughout this project—especially Joe Brooks, whose book title can't be beat, which is why I borrowed it.

Bass Bug Fishing

The Bass-Bug Moment

"Fly-rod fishing for bass, and particularly bass-bug fishing, is the most difficult form of fresh-water angling."
 John Alden Knight, *Black Bass* (1949)

"I suppose the peculiar fascination bass bugging has is in the strike. To see a heavy fish rise from under the lily pads or slip out from under a dense growth of weeds to smash at a floating bug is the most tense moment an angler can experience at the end of any search."
 A. J. McClane, *The Practical Fly Fisherman* (1953)

"I have done my share of both trout and saltwater fishing, but there's just nothing to equal that heart-stopping eruption of water when one of these fellows, even a small one, grabs my bug."
 Jack Ellis, *Bassin' With a Fly Rod* (1996)

My father and I managed to keep Lake Winnipesaukee a family secret for nearly two decades—or so we preferred to think.

Of course, landlocked salmon and lake trout fishermen had always known about Winnipesaukee's cold, clean, deep, fertile waters, and bustling ice-fishing villages popped up on its surface every winter. The lakeside resort towns of Wolfeboro and Laconia had prospered for a hundred years because of the boating and swimming at Winnipesaukee, and summer homes ranging from modest cottages to million-dollar showcases dotted its shoreline and islands.

Winnipesaukee was—and still is—the biggest and best-known lake in New Hampshire, one of the most popular vacation destinations in all of New England. It wasn't *that* kind of secret.

What Dad and I knew that few others seemed to know—or to care about if they did—was that smallmouth bass grew big and abundant in Winnipesaukee, and that for a month or so in the late spring they moved into the shallows, where a father and son armed with fly rods and bass bugs could catch them from a canoe.

I mean, we could catch *lots* of them. Whenever Dad and I launched his seventeen-foot square-ended aluminum canoe at the sand beach for an afternoon of smallmouth bugging on Winnipesaukee, my mother demanded that we bring home a detailed report. So we tried to keep count. But sometimes we lost track and had to file an estimate (which, however, we presented as if it were precise, because Mum insisted on precision). Forty or fifty bass (we'd report "fifty-three" or "forty-seven" to make it sound as if we'd kept a conscientious count) made a good— but not particularly unusual—day, and if a few of them weren't three- or four-pounders, we were a little disappointed.

Many a small Tapply grandchild's first fly-rod fish was a hard-pulling smallmouth that had eaten a streamer dragged behind Grampa's canoe on Winnipesaukee.

I grew up casting deerhair bugs for bass, both largemouths and smallmouths, in lakes, ponds, and rivers all over New England. It was my favorite kind of fishing—even better, I thought, than casting dry

This smallmouth took a Tap's Bug.

flies to rising trout, or trolling streamer flies for landlocked salmon, or fishing for any trophy that lived in the ocean.

In every kind of fishing there is The Moment. With trout, it's when a fish tips up to sip in a dry fly. With salmon and tarpon, it's that first catapulting leap into the air. When I fished with bait, as I did obsessively as a kid, The Moment came at the first shuddering jiggle of the bobber or the first twitch of the line before it began to slither out through the guides.

The best fishing times are those visible moments of connection, and once you've stored enough of them away in your memory bank, they keep you focused and happy while you're getting skunked.

With bass, The Moment comes when the flat, dark, early-evening water against a fallen tree or beside a boulder or alongside a patch of lily pads or under an overhanging bankside bush suddenly implodes where an instant earlier a bass bug had been quietly resting.

Despite James A. Henshall's famous claim for bass, "Inch for inch and pound for pound, the gamest fish that swims," once you've tied in to comparably sized trout or salmon—or any saltwater gamefish—you know that freshwater bass are not exceptionally swift swimmers or strong fighters or athletic leapers.

But nothing in the universe of fishing can beat the thrilling topwater strike of a big bass. It's the visible moment of connection, the moment that proves you have *fooled* him, the moment when all the predatory pugnacity of the fish exposes itself. It's a primitive, primal moment for fish and angler alike. I shiver at the memory of it. I'm sure it taps into a strand of my DNA that has survived for eons. It exposes *me* as a primitive hunter-gatherer still, a predator myself.

Fishing for bass on underwater lures and flies is—well, it's okay. Underwater techniques are surely effective, often deadly, and sometimes the only way to catch them. If catching fish were the main point of it, I would fish subsurface more often than I do. I've done plenty of it, actually—but hardly ever when the possibility of a topwater Moment was even remote.

Nowadays, when I go bass fishing, I cast floating bugs to shoreline targets. If I can't do that, I rarely go bass fishing. This is not snobbishness or purism. It's just what I love to do.

My earliest bass Moments came on the Charles River. It was urban angling, close enough to our eastern Massachusetts suburban home to give us a few good hours on any promising summer's evening after Dad got home from the office. As the song goes, I loved that dirty water. We fished the Charles within the shadow of the venerable Waltham Watch Factory. There the river broadens and moves with no discernible current whatsoever. There are weedy coves and miles of irregular brush-clogged shoreline featuring sunken trees and banks that drop abruptly

The Bass-Bug Moment.

to the water—delicious largemouth cover, and one great target after another for the bass-bug fly caster.

In order to share the guiding duties equally, Dad and I flipped a coin to decide who'd start out casting, and then we played the game of "three-strikes-and-you're-out." Our rules were simple: If you caught a bass, regardless of his size, you turned the rod over to your partner and took up the paddle. Or if you missed three strikes that the man with the paddle—who acted as autocratic umpire—declared were bass, you gave up your turn. Because big bluegills and crappies and an occasional pickerel also lived in the Charles, good-natured disputes sometimes arose. If the fishing was fast, the paddler tended to be more forgiving in his verdicts. When strikes came slowly and the paddler felt it was about time for a real fisherman to take up the rod, he'd yell "Bass!" at any swirl or splash at the bug.

We played three-and-out on the nearby Sudbury and Concord Rivers, too, and on dozens of lakes, ponds, reservoirs, and rivers both close to home and scattered across New England—Vermont's Lake Champlain, the Belgrade Lakes in Maine, the Quabbin in central Massachusetts, dozens of kettle ponds on Cape Cod, unnamed back-

When playing "three-strikes-and-you're-out," any bass counts, regardless of its size.

water sloughs of the Merrimack and Connecticut Rivers, and countless hidden New Hampshire ponds accessible only by a long portage through the woods.

Every summer while I was growing up, we took our two-week family vacation at a rented cabin on a smallmouth lake in Maine or New Hampshire. We swam and boated and trolled lazily during the day, my mother and sister and father and I, but after supper, Dad and I set off alone in the boat and headed for a rocky shoal or a boulder-strewn shoreline for a few hours of serious evening bugging.

Bass fishing—and the fun and effectiveness of casting floating bugs for them with a fly rod—was, of course, no secret. Dr. James A. Henshall published his *Book of the Black Bass* in 1881, and Ernest Peckinpaugh's Night Bug, which he invented in 1911 and which was mass-produced soon thereafter, was the result of a long evolutionary process. Dozens of books and hundreds of magazine articles have glorified bug fishing since then.

But the only fly-rod bass anglers I saw when I was a kid were those I shared a boat with. In fact, my father and I rarely encountered other bass fishermen, even on the lakes and rivers in the densely populated metropolitan area where we lived. When we did, they were usually

---

The author's mother took this smallmouth on a Maine lake.

solitary cigar-chomping men anchored or adrift in wooden rowboats, quietly casting Jitterbugs or Hula Poppers toward the shore or watching a live minnow tow a big red-and-white bobber around a weedy cove. These men were as low-tech as we were, and we always waved and gave them wide berth.

In the mid-1960s, my parents retired to central New Hampshire—a location chosen specifically for its proximity to good grouse hunting and one of the best smallmouth lakes in New England, so that Dad could continue to do what he'd always loved the most.

It was an inspired choice. Nowhere had we ever found bass fishing as dependable as what we had on Winnipesaukee—and it was just a two-minute drive from his house on the hilltop in East Alton.

Experience had taught us that about six weeks after ice-out, sometime in late May, the bass moved into the shallows to spawn. In the first week or two of it, we caught bass of all sizes—big females swollen with roe mixed in with the smaller, more abundant and aggressive males. As the spawning season progressed, the larger fish came less regularly, and then usually to a streamer trolled over deeper water. After about a month, their spawning completed for the year, the smallmouths retreated from the shallows, and the fast midday bass bugging was over for another year.

This was simple, unencumbered angling—an aluminum canoe with a small Evinrude mounted on the transom, a paddle, two fly rods, a box of flies, a spool of tippet, and a pair of needle-nose pliers equipped us fully. The man in the bow cast simple deerhair bugs to shoreline targets—jumbles of boulders, boat docks, overhanging brush, fallen trees, and, especially, the big round white-gravel spawning beds that stood out clearly through polarized sunglasses—while the stern man, either running the motor at super-slow or paddling parallel to an attractive shaded shoreline, trolled a streamer. We never had to travel far from the sand beach where we put in. We had our favorite hot spots, of course, but most of the lake's shoreline swarmed with smallmouths in late May and early June.

We didn't hoard our secret or disguise our intentions. Anybody who chose to spy on us could have learned our methods, and he would have seen a lot of bent fly rods. But the fact is that for the first decade or so after his retirement, my father and I seemed to be the only bass fishermen on Winnipesaukee.

Everything changed for us one pretty June afternoon about twenty years ago.

Dad had called a few days earlier. "They're on the beds," he said.

"See you Thursday," I answered.

That was, as usual, the entire conversation between a pair of old fishing partners.

Thursday morning I drove north from my home in eastern Massachusetts to the house in East Alton. Dad had the canoe already lashed to the roof of his wagon, with the motor and paddle and a couple of fly rods and a box of bugs stowed in back.

We launched at the sand beach and chugged toward the first island, our traditional starting point.

Then we saw the bass boats circling our island. There were three or four of them moving along the same path and at the same electric-trolling-motor speed, as if they were all grooved on some invisible track. Each boat featured two or three pedestal seats, and perched on every seat was a fisherman armed with a spinning or bait-casting rod. They were raking the shoreline of that little island. It was hard to imagine that they missed dragging a lure past a single underwater rock, or that they failed to jab a treble hook into the mouth of a single one of the short-tempered bass that always gathered around the island in spawning time.

The second island was the same, and so was the shaded shoreline by the girls' camp. In fact, that afternoon we found bass boats sitting in every cove and drifting over every underwater shoal and creeping along every shore that we visited.

It was my first encounter with a bass tournament.

Those boats were admirable craft, sleek and glitter-painted, designed specifically for bass fishing. Giant outboards hung off their transoms to get those fishermen where they wanted to go without wasting any time. Foot-operated electric motors up in the bow enabled them to cast and steer at the same time. The boats featured electronic fishfinders, live wells, lure boxes the size of steamer trunks, and whole arsenals of spinning and bait-casting rods.

Those fishermen threw and cranked, and they did haul in bass. As Dad and I putted past in our hopelessly old-fashioned canoe, we couldn't help admiring their efficiency. Throw, crank, haul back, set hook, shout, reel in, thumb bottom lip, hold aloft, admire, unhook, toss overboard, throw, crank. . . .

They had it down to a science, we could see that. If Dad and I might catch fifty bass on a soft June day, a boatload of these guys looked like they could catch a hundred or more.

We never made a single cast that day. We figured that any shoreline or island we might find vacant had already been raked thoroughly. So we turned around and headed back to the sand beach.

That afternoon we went trout fishing.

The bass-boat revolution, of course, had been under way for many years before we ran into that tournament on Winnipesaukee. Spinning became popular shortly after World War II, and it quickly democratized fishing. With spinning gear, anyone could make a long, smooth cast on his first try, with none of those backlashes that plagued levelwind bait casters or any of that awkward back-and-forth flailing that frustrated the beginning fly caster.

Spinning gave fishing to the people, and bass, particularly large-mouths, were the people's fish. By the middle of this century, bass thrived all over the country. Almost every body of warm fresh water held bass. They were accessible and abundant, and they grew big. They were aggressive and impetuous, unlike the moody trout. Bass were blue-collar fish; trout were high-society. In a barroom brawl, you'd put your money on any bass over the toughest trout in the joint.

I suppose it's entirely consistent with the American spirit that bass fishing would become a competitive sport and a big business. The Bass Anglers Sportsman Society (B.A.S.S.) was founded in the 1960s, and soon Jimmy Houston and Roland Martin and Bill Dance became household names. Industries competed with each other to invent artificial lures that bass would eat. Bass lures were called "baits," and they had down-to-earth designations—plastic worms and jig-and-pigs, stickbaits and buzzbaits and spinnerbaits. They were made of rubber and plastic and metal, and they came in myriad colors, many of which could be found nowhere in nature, but which, their creators claimed, drove bass nuts. They all worked, of course. Bass eat anything. But an endorsement from a bass champion guaranteed big sales.

Other enterprising businessmen designed boats and motors and electronics specifically for bass fishermen. They adapted space-age materials to the construction of lines, rods, and reels, and addicted bassmen bought that stuff, too.

With money on the line, competitive bass fishermen began to study the habits of their quarry and the ways that bass behavior correlated with season and weather and water temperature and other variables. They studied the habits and behavior of bass prey, too, so they could imitate them with the shape, color, size, and action of their lures. They made a science of bass fishing. And they sure could catch 'em.

Inevitably, tournament bass fishing spread north and west until, by the late 1970s or so, bass clubs were sponsoring contests all over the country. Recreational, noncompetitive bass fishing, of course, mirrored the exploding popularity of the tournaments. For every competitive pro, there were hundreds of amateurs who trailered boats, hunted bass obsessively with spinning rods, and dreamed of joining the tournament circuit.

Dad and I were probably lucky not to have encountered the bass boats earlier.

I blame high-tech bassing for the decline in smallmouth fishing on Winnipesaukee—or at least for the decline in my enjoyment of it. I have no evidence that competitive bassmen injure or kill the fish they catch, and maybe they don't drive the bass off their spawning beds or otherwise discourage them from hitting bass bugs, although that's how it seems. But I do not like feeling that the water I want to fish has already been combed with treble hooks or that I have no secrets, and I resent the fact that our bass lake is now publicized on Saturday-morning cable television. When I go fishing, I don't like crowds.

To give the bassmen credit, professional bassin' has produced a new emphasis on catch-and-release and other conservation practices, and it's been the impetus for important scientific studies of bass habitat and behavior. All sportsmen should be grateful for that, and fly fishermen, if they're so inclined, can use this lore to catch more bass themselves.

Anyway, who am I to define somebody else's fun?

My kids think I'm hopelessly old-fashioned. "Out-of-it" is their term, and I'm inclined to agree with them. I tell them I know what I like, and I admit I'm probably too old and set in my ways to change even if I wanted to. I just happen to love fly-rod bass-bug fishing.

Native Americans practiced a version of bass bugging before Europeans invaded the continent. Lobbing out something big and buggy with a long pole and dragging it across the surface of a warm-water pond, lake, or creek was an American invention, and the first way bass were caught. So I guess I *am* old-fashioned.

It's really quite simple: I love casting deerhair bass bugs into the shaded holes next to fallen trees on a summer's evening around that magical time when the sun has dipped behind the hills and the sky is turning purple and a fuzzy mist hovers over my pond, when the nighthawks and bats and swallows begin to swoop and dart over the water, when its surface lies as flat and smooth as a pane of black glass, when all is silent except for the grump of a bullfrog, the creak of an oar-lock or dip of a paddle, and the occasional spat of a bluegill, when I am alone in a canoe or a leaky rowboat or a float tube, or maybe in the company of a comfortable old like-minded partner who doesn't need to talk to be companionable, when my bug lands with a muffled splat, sits there long enough for the rings to widen and disappear, and then goes ploop, burble, and glug when I give it a few tugs before letting it rest some more, and when, always at the unexpected moment no matter how keen my anticipation, the silence and the water's mirrored surface—and my nerves—are shattered by the explosive ker-SLOSH of a big bass.

For me, this is the best way to fish for them.

Actually, it's the best way to fish for almost everything, provided we define "best" as "most fun," and not necessarily "most efficient." The only reason to fish for bluegills with anything but miniature top-water bass bugs is if you need to catch three bushels of them instead of only two. Pike and pickerel, which tend to lurk in bassy shallow-water places, eagerly devour big, noisy topwater bugs, and the savagery of their attack is, if anything, more heart-stopping than that of a bass. Topwater fly fishing for bluefish and striped bass and other saltwater predators produces similar results—often from fish that weigh twenty pounds or more. I've caught six-pound Labrador brook trout on hair mice dragged across a current—and even on generic deerhair bugs twitched past beds of lily pads. "Bombers" and similar deerhair bugs, waked across the currents, are proven Atlantic salmon killers.

Bugging with a fly rod may not be the best way to catch the most bass, or to catch the biggest bass, although I'm convinced that sometimes it is. On a few occasions, I've been manipulated into trying to prove it—which I've done, at least to my own satisfaction. But "most" and "biggest" are competitive terms, and they don't interest me.

Fishing for bass with deerhair bugs is straightforward and simple, but it's not simplistic. It may be less than science, but it's more than random luck. Doing it right and doing it well involve practice and knowledge and experience. Luck, of course, also helps.

Bass, God bless 'em, do not behave with the absolute predictability that experts sometimes attribute to them. I'm not sure that bass have free will, and I readily acknowledge that they exhibit predictable *tendencies.* At different seasons and under different weather conditions, they *tend* to gather in particular types of water, and at any given time their collective moods *tend* to cluster somewhere along a spectrum from aggressive to closemouthed. Computers can factor in all the variables and spit out reliable generalizations. Many helpful books have been written on these subjects. You can use the data to help you decide whether you want to go fishing, and if you do, where to park your boat and what to tie onto your leader.

Or you can just look out the window, sniff the air, and decide that it feels right. That's generally what I do. And even when it feels wrong, if you have the urge to spend some time on the water, that's always a good time to go fishing. Even under the least-favorable conditions, you can usually find a few ornery bass that will refuse to be predictable and that will engulf a bass bug when they're not supposed to.

It's true: The best time to go fishing is whenever you can. But there are times of the day and the season when bass bugging can be absolutely magical. Go at these times if you can.

You'll have more fun—and catch more bass—if you know what you're doing and if you can do it right.

It starts with the bug you choose to tie onto your tippet. Not all bass bugs are equal. Many fly rodders disagree with me, but I believe that soft-bodied bugs made from spun deerhair and other lifelike materials are superior in almost all respects to hard-bodied cork, balsa, or plastic lures. Some deerhair designs work better than others. The most fun of all is catching bass on bugs you've created and made yourself—an element of bass fishing that the spin- and bait-casting guys miss completely. If you prefer model building to fly tying, you should by all means construct and fish with balsa or cork bugs. You will catch plenty of bass.

The bug must be cast to places where bass are likely to be lurking. Recognizing these places demands knowledge and imagination and some understanding of your quarry. Consistently accurate casting is the product of practice and well-balanced equipment.

These are some of the matters we'll look at in this book.

Soon after that June day when Dad and I encountered the bass tournament on Winnipesaukee, I began to find bass boats on the Charles and Concord Rivers and just about every lake, pond, and river where a truck could back a trailered boat down to the water. Many times I launched myself in my canoe or float tube and paddled along a good shoreline without a strike, and I just knew that someone had beaten me to it. More often than not, I found a bass boat anchored in my favorite cove around the point, confirming my suspicions. Then the only thing to do was turn around and paddle back.

Pretty soon, I just assumed that a bass boat had already raked the shoreline I intended to fish. I was discouraged even before I made a cast—sometimes so discouraged that I changed my mind and stayed home. Negative thinking, I know.

My secret hot spots were no longer secret. What had taken me years of exploration, trial, and error to discover, those smart modern bassmen, with the help of their electronics and science, had figured out instantly.

If it sounds like I resented them . . . well, I did. When you've hoarded wonderful "secrets" like Lake Winnipesaukee and the Charles River all your life, you don't surrender them gracefully.

As a matter of fact, it was so discouraging that I briefly quit bass bugging entirely.

But all those memories of implosive swirls shattering the stillness of a summer evening, those Moments of connection with a big bass, continued to haunt me.

I knew I couldn't beat the men in bass boats. They always got there quicker and covered the water more efficiently than I could. But I did fish with some of them, and I learned from them, and I added what I learned to what I already knew about the special magic of bass-bug fishing.

And I began exploring for new bass water, places without concrete boat launches. I collected new secrets, and I learned how to coexist with my high-tech counterparts.

I may not catch as many bass as the bass-boat/spinning-rod guys do, and those I catch may not be as big. But I catch enough, and they're big enough, to convince me that casting deerhair bugs with a fly rod is still the best way to fish for bass.

2

From Bobs to Bugs

"Happening to have a fish-hook in my pocket, I cut off a piece of the deer's tail, and made a 'bob.' Then, cutting a long, slender pole, and tying the bob to the end with a piece of strong twine some three feet long, we got into the boat, my comrade paddling and I manipulating the bob."
James A. Henshall, *Book of the Black Bass* (1881)

"From the standpoint of durability and easy casting, nothing so far developed is superior to the Henshall type [of bug]."
J. Edson Leonard, *Flies* (1950)

"Bass-bugging is a type of fly-rod fishing that was born and raised right here in America. Considering that most fly fishing dates well back into English history, it's a young sport, young enough that as a boy I was among the first to fish these big bugs in this way."
Ray Bergman, *Fishing with Ray Bergman* (1970)

Anglers who care about tradition—and who among us doesn't?—will be comforted to know that bass bugging is probably the oldest method of catching fish on hook and line in North America. In 1741, when William Bartram described how Florida's Seminole Indians fooled largemouth bass (which he called "trout") with a "bob," it's likely he was reporting on an angling method that had been practiced for generations before the Europeans invaded the continent.

"Two people are in a little canoe," wrote Bartram, "one sitting in the stern to steer, and the other near the bow, having a rod ten or twelve feet in length, to one end of which is tied a strong line, about twenty inches in length, to which is fastened three large hooks, back to back. These are fixed very securely, and tied with the white hair of a deer's tail, shreds of a red garter, and some particoloured feathers, all which form a tuft or tassel nearly as large as one's fist, and entirely cover and conceal the hooks; that is called a 'bob.' The steersman paddles softly, and proceeds slowly along shore, keeping parallel to it, at a distance just sufficient to admit the fisherman to reach the edge of the floating weeds along shore; he now ingeniously swings the bob backwards and forwards, just above the surface and sometimes tips the water with it; when the unfortunate cheated trout [sic] instantly springs from under the weeds and seizes the prey."

Bass bugging has always been effective. It's doubtful if the Seminoles were much interested in sport or artfulness. They needed fish to eat, and Everglades largemouths were their most available species. So if bob fishing hadn't been an efficient way of capturing them—no matter how much fun it was—they undoubtedly would have developed a deadlier method.

Today when we rig up our graphite fly rods and cast our sleek hair-and-feather concoctions onto the water for bass, we are practicing an ancient and uniquely American technique that takes advantage of the bass's aggressive surface-feeding habits. Modern bass bugs—and the methods by which they are fished—are mere refinements of angling with the primitive bob.

By the middle of the nineteenth century, bob fishing had expanded northward into North Carolina, whose natives refined the lure into something that resembled our modern deerhair bug. In *Flies*, J. Edson Leonard explained how bobs were made from squares of deerskin ("preferably from the skin from the shin bones"), which were cured, cut into strips "about the width of a shoe string," and soaked to make them pliable. "With the tail fastened on," wrote Leonard, "there remains only to tie the body in place and fasten on the wings. Taper one edge of the strip and tie it to the shank. Wind the strip around the shank, fasten it with the working silk, tie on the wings and the bug will be complete. The hair will project nearly at right angles to the body and will weave back and forth when the bug is retrieved." This version of the bob, as the Native bass anglers undoubtedly understood, covers the bend of the hook with bristly deerhair, making it virtually weedless.

Most early European Americans persisted in fishing for bass as their Old World traditions had taught them to fish for trout and salmon. There is no evidence that non-native American anglers designed a single fly—topwater or subsurface—specifically for bass before the late 1800s. All of the "bass flies" described and pictured in Mary Orvis Marbury's classic *Favorite Flies and Their Histories*, published in 1892, are simply larger and generally gaudier versions of the hackle-

and-feather wet flies that Charles Cotton had written about two centuries earlier—or, for that matter, Dame Juliana before him.

Still, the effectiveness of topwater fishing for bass with a fly was well known. Those hackle-and-feather "bass flies" were typically fished on or near the surface. Henshall, in an 1880 magazine article, wrote: "The angler should endeavor to cast his flies as lightly as possible, causing them to settle as quietly as possible, and without a splash. After casting, the flies should be skipped along the surface in slightly curving lines, or by zigzag movements, occasionally allowing them to become submerged for several inches near likely-looking spots. If the current is swift, allow the flies to float naturally with it, at times, when they can be skittered back again, or withdrawn for a new cast."

That sounds a lot like bass bugging to me.

In his *Book of the Black Bass*, the only flies Henshall mentioned were those same colorful and oversized trout and salmon flies. Whether he actually invented the spun deerhair bug that bears his name, or whether the so-called Henshall Bug was invented by somebody else and named after the father of American bass fishing, is uncertain. J. Edson Leonard gives the doctor full credit. "Dr. James A. Henshall did more, perhaps, to exploit the first bass hair bugs than any other angler," Leonard wrote. "He is credited with having made the original hair bug, one which bears his name to this day." Jack Ellis, on the other hand, says: "The Buckhair Mouse and the Henshall Bug, widely marketed by the Weber Life-Like Fly Company . . . were based on [Orley] Tuttle's [1919] creation."

Matthew Hodgson, a lifelong collector of bass bugs and bass-bug lore, concurs with Leonard. "The so-called Henshall bugs preceded cork-bodied bugs by about a decade," says Hodgson. "Henshall named the various patterns after, among others, some heroes of the Spanish-American War. Others he named for outdoor writers—O. W. Smith, et al. —who wrote during the 1910–25 period. Amusingly, the 'Henshall's Own' pattern originally was a patriotic red, white, and blue. When it failed to catch many bass, he adopted a more drab coloration for his 'personal pattern.'"

In *Fly-Tying* (1940), William Bayard Sturgis credits Chicagoans Emerson Hough and Fred Peet—not Dr. Henshall—with "inventing" the spun-deerhair body in 1912. According to Sturgis, Hough and Peet "worked on the development of this fly for the better part of one winter. They eventually evolved one which was named the 'Emerson Hough.' The original pattern, as created by these two gentlemen, was made entirely from bucktail." It's likely that since bucktail is not hollow, Hough and Peet intended their fly to be fished wet. The logical next step—spinning the hollow body hair of deer to create a bug that

Henshall Bug.

would float—apparently came somewhat later. Sturgis and others describe a number of floating "moth" bugs with spun deerhair bodies. His Algoma featured a slender spun-and-clipped deerhair body, a bucktail overwing, and several turns of hackle at the head. The Emerson Hough is identical (when spun deerhair instead of bucktail is used for the body), except this fly omits the Algoma's front hackle.

The Henshall Bug simply substituted a pair of bucktail wings on the sides for the single wing over the back. It featured a tail of bucktail—white in the middle with a contrasting color on each side—flanked by splayed grizzly feathers. The body was built from spun-and-clipped natural deerhair, typically with a colorful stripe around its middle. The wings were fashioned from a bunch of bucktail tied in a downwing style over the clipped-deerhair body and then divided and figure-eighted into position so that they stuck out at right angles near the front of the hook.

In fact, little has changed in the design of deerhair bugs since the Emerson Hough, the Algoma, and the Henshall Bugs, and while their air-resistant wings make them somewhat unwieldy to cast (although a

9- or 10-weight outfit can throw them pretty well), all of them will take bass as well as any sleek contemporary design.

Regardless of who invented the Henshall Bug and when it happened, bass bugging remained an obscure technique through the nineteenth century, practiced, as far as we know, only by bob fishermen. The term "bass-bug fishing" had not even been coined.

"Shortly after the turn of the century," writes Paul Schullery in *American Fly Fishing*, "the bass bug experienced a startling growth in popularity, and most of the enduring forms were created. There have been hundreds, perhaps even thousands, but they follow a few main types."

The sudden popularity of bass-bug fishing resulted from two related factors. First, the effectiveness of high-floating cork and wood bodies, in combination with feathers and other decorations, was discovered. Second, unlike deerhair, cork and wood were durable, easy-to-work-with materials that could be—and soon were—mass-produced.

In 1900, not a single commercially made bass bug could be pur-chased. By the 1930s, Schullery reports, "there was a bewildering assortment of bass bugs available, possibly even more than there are today." It wasn't so much that bass fishermen created a demand for commercially manufactured bugs. Rather, the production, distri-bution, and marketing of bugs created the sport of bass bugging. Designers such as Ernest Peckinpaugh and Cal McCarthy, manufac-turers such as B. F. Wilder, and sporting writers such as Will H. Dilg worked together—and competed against each other—to popularize what had been a virtually unknown sport, and to create a burgeoning market for their products.

Prototypes of the commercial cork-bodied bass bug had been used by the backcountry "swampers" of Arkansas and Missouri, who lashed beer-bottle corks and turkey feathers to a hook and caught bass on them before the turn of the century.

It's uncertain who deserves credit for the first commercial bass bug. Schullery gives the nod to William Jamison of Chicago, whose Coaxer (wide, flat cork body, red felt wings, and feather tail lying flat over the top of the hook) was created around 1910. A. J. McClane nom-inates Tennessean Ernest Peckinpaugh, whose Night Bug (feathers, bucktail, and a double hook, all lashed to a cork stopper) was manu-factured by the John J. Hildebrandt Company and popularized in sporting magazines by Will H. Dilg.

Jack Ellis contends that the first fly-rod popper was invented by none other than trout legend Theodore Gordon, but that fly-rod bass-ing was held in such low esteem among dry-fly anglers of the time that to protect Gordon's reputation and preserve his shameful secret (he fished for bass!), he and his contemporaries deflected credit for inventing the lowly bass bug to Peckinpaugh.

In any case, by 1930, with considerable help from Dilg and the Hildebrandt Company, Peckinpaugh had become the name most intimately associated with bass bugs. Dozens of variations of "Peck's Bugs" were made available in a highly competitive market.

Toward the end of his life, Peckinpaugh reflected on his first creation, the Night Bug. "I discovered that late in the afternoon," he wrote, "and at dusk, if I could keep a bucktail fly on top of the water, I would catch more fish. This gave me the idea of putting a cork on a hook, and tying the bucktail hair to the lure, and in that way making it stay on the surface. A little experimenting quickly showed me that a single hook could not be securely fastened to the cork, but I did find that by using a double hook, I could make a very solid bug. Therefore, all the first bass bugs I made were on double hooks. These bugs were designed for taking bream. I found that just before dark the bream would strike on the surface and I could catch them by using one of these little cork body bugs.

"There was practically no further development in these bugs until 1910 or 1911. I am uncertain about which year. Anyway, at this particular time, my work as a contractor kept me pretty busy and the jobs were always so far away from home that they interfered considerably with my usual periods of fishing. By the time I arrived at one of the lakes or ponds where I usually fished, it would be just about dark, so I was compelled to fish at night. I then discovered that bass would strike the same bugs which I had been using for bream. But the hook was small and I lost most of the fish. This inspired me to make a larger edition of the double hook bugs, and inasmuch as they were developed for night fishing, I called them 'Night Bugs.' I made these bass bugs in many colors of feathers and bucktail hair."

Matt Hodgson speculates that "Peck chose cork for his original bass bugs because of the silk fly lines of his day, which sank after an hour or two, dragging hair bugs beneath the surface of the water, while cork- (or wood-) bodied bugs tended to float for long periods." Hodgson notes that Peckinpaugh also made unsinkable bugs from red cedar.

When the Great War broke out in Europe in 1914, Peckinpaugh lost his British source of double hooks and was forced to adapt his Night Bug to the single hook. He tied for friends and sold them locally in Chattanooga. Bass-fishing tourists bought them, and thus Peckinpaugh's bugs migrated to other parts of the country and eventually to those who would make them for the market, although, as Hodgson points out, "Peck made a fairly full line of bass bugs before South Bend, Heddon, et al., put their bugs on the market."

Peckinpaugh experimented with a variety of designs and concluded that flat-faced bugs with horizontal notches were most effective for catching bass. "After a time, however," remembers Hodgson, "he gave his 'popping minnows' concave faces simply because the public demanded this design. Until his company closed, he still made a number of bugs with the horizontal-notched faces."

Other popular cork-bodied bugs of the 1920s and 1930s were the Cal-Mac Moth, a flat-winged affair devised by Cal McCarthy, and the Wilder-Dilg, the prototype for the still-popular "feathered minnow," which featured a pointed nose, a bullet-shaped body, wound hackle at the butt, and a long tail of hackle feathers.

"Possibly the single most important popularizer of bass bugs was Will Dilg, who wrote for *Outing Recreation*," notes Matt Hodgson. "Dilg wrote numerous articles—particularly about the 'Mississippi Bass Bugs.' Cal McCarthy, while a great caster and a good bug maker, never contributed much that was original."

Around this time, Tom Loving of Baltimore invented his Gerbubble Bug, which Joe Brooks called "the best largemouth bug I've ever used." Loving's creation featured hackle feathers inserted into slits cut along both sides of the cork body so that the fibers stuck out perpendicular to the hook shank, creating the effect of dozens of legs kicking at the water's surface.

Meanwhile, fly tiers were busy creating their own deerhair counterparts of the commercial cork-bodied bugs. In 1919, Orley Tuttle designed a deerhair "bug" to imitate the beetles he saw smallmouths eating on his local lake. Instead of spinning deerhair onto the hook as Henshall had done, Tuttle laid bunches of hair parallel to the hook shank and lashed them down fore and aft, clipping the front into a stubby head and leaving the tips of the hair to flare around the bend of the hook.

When Tuttle showed his outlandish creation to his wife, as the story goes, she declared: "Looks like the devil to me." And thus it was named the Devil Bug.

So hungry were bass-bug anglers for new lures that by 1922, Tuttle was selling fifty thousand bugs a year in over eight hundred combinations of color, size, and design—moth bugs, beetle bugs, mouse bugs, and even a baby duck Devil Bug. If (as Jack Ellis claims) Dr. Henshall did not invent the Henshall Bug, credit for the first deerhair bass bug almost certainly goes to Tuttle. In any case, the Devil Bug was the first commercial deerhair bass bug.

In the 1930s, Joe Messinger elevated the tying of deerhair bugs to an art form. He crafted his realistic and utterly elegant frogs by stacking rather than spinning the deerhair body. This technique involved holding a bundle of hair in place to prevent it from twirling 360 degrees around the shank of the hook as he drew the thread tight over it to

Messinger Frog.

make it flare. In this way, Messinger created two-toned clipped deer-hair frogs with pale bellies and green backs. To make protruding, kicking legs, he inserted a piece of wire into a bunch of two-toned bucktail, wound over the knees with thread, bent the wire into shape, and fixed the joints with glue.

When spinning arrived in North America in the 1940s, it produced a decline in the popularity of fly fishing in general and in fly fishing for bass in particular. Jack Ellis refers to the first three postwar decades as the "Dark Age" of bass-bug fishing. Typical of the new attitude toward fly fishing for bass was that of Jason Lucas, who wrote in 1947: "Bass bugging is an extremely crude form of fly fishing, if fly fishing it can be called. . . . A child of average mentality should learn bass bugging in a few minutes." Bass fishing, under the influence of Lucas and many others, was becoming a science for spin and bait casters, and while it wasn't to become apparent until sometime in the 1970s, the bass-boat/high-tech/big-money tournament revolution had begun.

Hard-bodied fly-rod bugs continued to be manufactured during the postwar years, and new materials such as foam and molded plastic were introduced. But the designs didn't change, because creative energies shifted to lures that could be cast with spinning and bait-casting outfits. That particular market was exploding.

A few stalwart fly fishermen continued to experiment with hair-and-feather designs. Roy Yates created a deerhair version of the Wilder-Dilg feathered minnow—a design he adapted from Don Gapen's Muddler, and which he called the Deacon. Yates's Deacon featured a roundish white spun-and-clipped deerhair head; a white bucktail overwing; a red, yellow, or chartreuse floss body; and a flared yellow hackle feather tail. The Deacon floated low on the water, burbled subtly, and vibrated and rippled enticingly even at rest. Best of all was the fact that an angler could cast it as easily as a streamer fly with a midweight trout rod.

When I began bass bugging with my father in the 1950s, the Deacon was our bug of choice.

"Until Roy Yates sent me one of his Deacons," Dad recalls, "I mostly used a bait-casting rod and Jitterbugs or Magic Minnows or Johnson Spoons to catch bass. The Deacon converted me to fly-rod bass bugging, mainly because I found I could cast it comfortably on a 5- or 6-weight trout rod. I caught a lot of bass on the Deacon. But I kept wondering how I could improve it.

"The best feature of the Deacon was its streamlined shape. It cast as comfortably as a streamer fly. But I felt it didn't kick up enough of a fuss on the surface due to its little round head. And there wasn't enough clipped deerhair on it to keep it afloat very long. So I began experimenting."

Tap, like Roy Yates, was a minimalist, a tinkerer, and an inventor. He believed that bass don't care whether a lure imitates actual prey, and he doubted that they had any appreciation for artfulness whatsoever. So he sought to create a bug that would meet the *angler's* needs for a useful and effective bass bug. The ideal bass bug, Tap believed, would be durable, castable, and suggestive. It would "kick up a fuss" when twitched and retrieved, it would float well, it would feel soft and lifelike in the mouth of a fish, and it would be relatively simple to tie.

Tap's early efforts produced a remarkably close imitation of the original Henshall Bug (although I don't believe he was aware of it). It featured a full-length clipped-deerhair body, with a flat bottom and a wide, rounded front end tapered to a narrow waist at the rear of the hook. He left untrimmed deerhair whiskers on front and made a tail of flared hackle feathers. "I soon cut off those whiskers," he says. "Too air-resistant for pleasant casting, and they tended to twist the leader and make the bug land upside-down. Then to get the kind of burble I wanted, I left the face flat rather than rounding it off. I fiddled with the tail. The hackle feathers gave it a nice leggy action, but they made the thing whistle and spin when I cast it. Bucktail or long, fine deerhair works much better. It gives the bug the illusion of size without adding weight or air resistance. The secret to making one of these bugs is packing the spun deerhair really tight. The rest is all hedge clipping." He adds: "I can make one in about twenty minutes."

Dan Bailey produced and sold Tap's Bugs for many years, and fly-rod bassers, the relatively few of them who were still practicing the ancient art in that "Dark Age," liked them for all the reasons Dad had in mind when he created them. When he sent a handful to Charles F. Waterman in the 1970s, the author of *Fly Rodding for Bass* reported: "Last week we used your bugs, together with poppers, on Lake Okeechobee, and yours were winners by a considerable margin."

The pleasures of topwater fly rodding for bass were chronicled in books and magazines through the fifties, sixties, and seventies by that era's most respected fishing writers, notably Joe Brooks, John Alden Knight, A. J. McClane, Harold F. Blaisdell, Tom Nixon, Ray Bergman, H. G. Tapply, Charles Waterman, and Tom McNally. All of these esteemed angling gurus wrote fondly of fly-rod bass-bug fishing, but only Nixon fished for bass exclusively with the fly rod, and Brooks's book was the only one that focused exclusively on bass-bug fishing. The others all fished widely, for a variety of species, and with whatever tackle promised success. You could catch bass with fly-rod bugs, they insisted. But you could catch them other ways, too. As Bergman lamented, there seemed to be a "growing apathy toward fly fishing on the part of bass anglers."

So in the "Dark Age" of the postwar bass-boat revolution, bass bugging became a novelty in the popular mind, a harmless (and "crude") sport that was being kept alive by nostalgic old-timers who'd sometimes rather flail around with fly rods than catch a lot of bass.

The revival of bass-bug fishing—what Nick Lyons calls "the bass-fly revolution"—began in the 1970s and can be credited largely to the efforts of Dave Whitlock, who in Jack Ellis's words "made bass bugging respectable." Whitlock, says Ellis, "brought dignity, artistry, and class to bass bugging. . . . He was the first famous bass bugger (there's got to be a better term) in history who did not, with the lone exception of Messinger, occasionally use the casting rod." Whitlock's bass-fly designs—subsurface as well as topwater—are colorful, sleek, and altogether elegant, and he writes about fly-rod bassing with knowledgeable enthusiasm. "Fly fishing for bass," he says in the *L. L. Bean Fly Fishing for Bass Handbook*, "may well be the most exciting, pleasurable, and consistently rewarding method of fishing that exists today in North America. . . . Bass are terrific fun on a fly rod!"

Whitlock reports that he devised bass flies and developed fly-fishing techniques by "studying and adapting the successful methods of the saltwater fly fishers and the spin and baitcasting bass fishermen." If his deerhair bugs are, to my old eye, dressed with unnecessary and redundant appendages and decorations (his Whit Hair Bug Series, for example, are basic Tap's Bugs in a variety of color combinations, complete with eyes, multimaterial tails, glitter, and rubber legs), they have served the purposes of appealing to an ever-widening population of anglers and creating enthusiastic bass-bug addicts. Whitlock's various deerhair divers, underwater swimmers, bottom flies, and jigs look and behave more like actual bass prey than the metal and plastic counterparts favored by the tournament bassmen.

Whitlock's imitative hair-and-feather bass flies—along with his enthusiastic promotion of fly fishing for bass—have converted a generation of trout anglers, who are predisposed to the concept of imitation, to the fun of fly-rod bass fishing. His bugs and lures offer fly fishermen a valid option to virtually every lure the tournament bassers can throw with a spinning or bait-casting rod. For every stickbait and crankbait and jig and rubber worm, there is a corresponding Whitlock creation for the fly fisherman—the Whit Hair Bug, Mouserat, Wigglelegs Frog, Snakey, Eeelworm Streamer, Hare Water Pup, Chamois Spring Lizard, Haregrub, Water Snake, Golden Shiner, Water Dog, Sand Eel, Deerhair Gerbubble Bug . . . the list goes on.

Other contemporary bass bug inventors such as Larry Dahlberg, (best known for his innovative deerhair Diver), John Betts, Bob Clouser, Dick Stewart, A. D. Livingston, C. Boyd Pfeiffer, Art Scheck, and Jack Gartside have made important contributions to the Whitlock bass-bug revival. Respected angling writers like Nick Lyons and John Gierach chronicle the poetic joys of fly-rod bugging, and *Warmwater Fly Fishing* magazine devotes considerable space each issue to bass-bug tying and fishing techniques.

I don't believe we actually need an arsenal of imitative flies to catch bass, but for the sake of the sport of bass bugging, I'm glad we have them. Their variety gives us genuine respectability, the inspiration to experiment at the vise and on the water, and, when the fishing is slow, legitimate options to the old-fashioned hair bug.

But on a soft summer evening I'm usually quite content to tie on my father's streamlined version of a strip-skin bob, plop it near a fallen tree, watch the rings widen and dissipate before making it go ker-PLOOP, and wait for that sudden implosion of water. It reminds me that I am not that far removed from the Seminole Indians of the seventeenth century. I like to stay in touch with my roots.

3

How Bugs Work

"It is with some degree of trepidation that I approach the subject of artificial flies, for I am afraid that I hold some very heretical notions on the subject. But of one fact I am positively convinced, and that is, that there is a good deal of humbug in this matter."

James A. Henshall, *Book of the Black Bass* (1881)

"If you'll learn to use bass bugs correctly you'll catch more fish than with any other type of lure. There's something about a bass bug that does things to a bass. Bugs make them mad."

Joe Brooks, *Bass Bug Fishing* (1947)

"Pattern is of minor importance in the deer-hair bugs."

Harold F. Blaisdell, *Tricks That Take Fish* (1954)

One of the reasons bass fishing has become so popular is that bass can—and do—thrive almost everywhere. You can catch bass in every one of the forty-eight contiguous states. Smallmouths coexist with lake trout and landlocked salmon in cold, deep northern lakes, and with rainbow, brown, and brook trout in quick-moving streams. Largemouths find virtually all warmwater lakes, ponds, reservoirs, rivers, creeks, and sloughs hospitable. About the only reason why a body of fresh water might not hold bass is because the fish have not found a way to migrate into it and nobody has yet dumped in a bucketful.

Bass live virtually everywhere for two reasons: They can tolerate a wide range of water conditions and temperatures, and they eat anything that moves and fits into their mouths.

The challenge for the bass fisherman is just this simple: Locate some water where bass live (almost everywhere), tie something to the end of your line (almost anything), cast it out there (however awkwardly), and make it move. Everything beyond that is refinement.

The more refined you become, of course, the more bass you'll catch.

Bass have evolved into finely tuned predators. They devote most of their lives to locating, stalking, catching, and devouring food. Efficient predators like bass hunt in places where their prey is most abundant and easiest to capture, and they eat whatever they happen to find there. A list of bass foods would really be an unabridged compendium of all creatures that live in and near water, but close to the top of any list would be shallow-water creatures—small fish of all species (including bass), frogs and other amphibians, insects, and various landlubbing critters.

The more vulnerable the prey, the better bass like it. Like all creatures, bass live by nature's equation: They survive and prosper when they can ingest the maximum nourishment with the minimum expenditure of energy. Bass are consistently found in shallow water because they find food there. Small baitfish tend to school in the cover of shoreline weeds. Frogs, salamanders, and other amphibians spend a lot of time in the water, but they never stray far from shore. Damselflies, dragonflies, and other aquatic insects hatch in or near shallow water. Terrestrial insects such as grasshoppers, beetles, crickets, caterpillars, and moths, as well as creatures like mice, moles, lizards, and worms, plop onto the water from the trees and grass that overhang the shoreline.

Bass seek cover so they can hide from their own predators while they lie in ambush for prey, and they want comfortable water temperatures and shelter from sources of discomfort such as bright sun. Usually, they find everything they want in shallow water. And because so much of their prey appears on or near the water's surface, bass are always looking up. If the water is clear enough for them to see to the surface, they'll happily shoot up ten or fifteen feet to hit something on top.

No doubt bass do most of their feeding underwater, because that's where they find their staples—baitfish, leeches, crayfish, and large nymphs. But they rarely refuse to feed off the top. In fact, bass understand that any prey appearing on the surface is usually out of its natural element and therefore more vulnerable and easier to catch than what lives underwater. A baitfish splashing on the surface must be injured or disoriented. Any insect or terrestrial creature that falls onto the water is quite helpless. Amphibians such as frogs are relatively poor swimmers, a nourishing bellyful, and no match for a hungry bass.

With bass, nothing is absolute. I've found river-dwelling small-mouths sipping windblown terrestrials or emerging mayflies as selectively as brown trout. Sometimes bass refuse to eat anything except a particularly abundant prey species such as soft-shelled crayfish. These are not productive times for the bass-bug fisherman.

But typically, bass are opportunistic feeders, on the prowl for a nourishing mouthful. Unlike trout anglers, bass-bug fishermen don't need to wait for and match a hatch to entice a fish to strike, nor do we need to imitate whatever a fish might have eaten most recently, or even what he's accustomed to finding in and on the water.

In fact, you don't need to imitate anything to catch bass consistently on bugs. Bass are confirmed opportunists. They go for anything that *suggests food.* "Bass," writes Paul Schullery, "are such admirable omnivores that they will eat almost anything if they're hungry, or disturbed, enough."

Bass hunt primarily by sight and sound. They can detect vibration and motion from long distances. If a grasshopper, dragonfly, moth, mouse, or frog—or bass bug—falls onto calm water and sits there twitching and struggling, every bass within twenty feet or so will hear it. If it sounds like it might be good to eat, at least one of them will swim over to investigate. Then, if it looks alive and nourishing—even if it looks like nothing he's ever seen before—he'll engulf it without bothering to inquire about its ancestry.

Bass are conditioned to assume that objects splatting onto the water and then wiggling, jerking, and chugging on the surface are good to eat. The closer those more or less lifelike objects splat down to them, the more likely they are to eat them. They prefer not to venture too far from their hiding places.

This is not to say that bass are always mindlessly aggressive, although often they appear to be exactly that. They're always alert for predators and quick to flee, in fact, and sometimes they seem to have little interest in eating. At such times, however, they can often be teased, seduced, angered, or tormented into striking.

During their spawning season, bass shift their attention from eating to protecting their territory, and they become, if anything, even more aggressive. Any alien that invades their sacred space—including a noisy bass bug—is, by their definition, an enemy that must be attacked and chased away or destroyed.

Pore through today's fly-fishing catalogs and you'll discover that topwater bass flies come in a bewildering variety of sizes, shapes, colors, and designs. There are poppers, chuggers, sliders, and divers made from deerhair, cork, balsa, hard and soft foam, silicone, synthetic tubing, and plastic. Many are clever and precise imitations of actual bass prey. They're typically decorated with lifelike arms, legs, wings, tails, fins, eyes, and gills. Some come equipped with propellers, rattlers, lips, and weedguards.

The unwary bass bugger might feel compelled to buy several of everything in each size and color available, on the theory that you never know what the bass might want at any given time on any particular body of water.

This theory often proves useful for trout fishermen. Trout really can be agonizingly selective.

But it's pretty much nonsense for the bass-bug angler. What bass usually "want" is something—anything—that's alive, easy to capture, and nourishing, and that's what—and *only* what—an effective bass bug needs to suggest to trigger the fish's predatory impulse.

Fancy, highly imitative bass bugs rarely catch more bass than generic, suggestive ones do, although they probably catch more fishermen. I do virtually all of my bass bugging with the deerhair creation my father invented nearly fifty years ago. Tap's Bug resembles no natural bass prey. Dad designed his bug to meet the needs of the fisherman, not the imagined appetites of bass. It's easy to tie, floats well, casts easily on midweight fly rods, and can be manipulated to burble, gurgle, ploop, and glug in ways that smallmouths and largemouths in all types of water consistently find irresistible.

Tap's Bug features a tightly packed deerhair body that's barbered to a triangular, aerodynamic shape, with a wide, flat face tapered back to the hind end. A deerhair tail suggests a bulky mouthful to a bass without actually being bulky. This bug has no arms, legs, or other appendages that would increase its air resistance and make it hard to cast. Dad doesn't bother with eyes, which are unquestionably fish attractors on underwater flies and lures but which are superfluous on topwater bugs, inasmuch as they'd be located above the water, where bass can't see them. He ties his bugs in whatever colors strike his fancy. Many bass buggers have faith in a particular color, but there's little evidence that the color of a surface bug makes the difference between a strike and a refusal.

Usually when I go bass bugging, I just tie on a Tap's Bug and fish with it all day unless a pickerel or pike tears it up or I bust it off in the bushes or in the mouth of a big bass. When that happens, I tie on another one.

Okay, when the fishing is particularly slow, or if I find myself in a whimsical mood, I sometimes do switch bugs. This makes me feel as if I'm doing something constructive, and I usually do it with a purpose in mind. When I do experiment with different bugs, I have logical reasons—but little science—for it.

If I'm in a fly-changing, problem-solving frame of mind, my choice of bugs depends less on imitating something I imagine the bass might want to eat than on the conditions I encounter on the water.

- In shallow, flat-calm water, I worry about my bug spooking fish when it hits the water. So I cast smallish soft-bodied bugs that land with a natural-sounding, quiet splat rather than a hard splash, and I prefer bugs with rounded faces that gurgle and burble seductively rather than flat faces that pop explosively.

- When I'm casting to small pockets and tight holes such as openings in a bed of lily pads or under overhanging bushes or among the limbs of waterlogged trees, where the bug must do its work without being moved away from the hot spot, I like a design that vibrates and wiggles when I give it the slightest twitch. Rubber arms and legs and hairy or splayed hackle feather or marabou tails give even a motionless bug subtle, lifelike action while it rests on the water.

- When a breeze riffles the surface, I tie on something big and loud to command a bass's attention—a flat-nosed deerhair bug or a hard-bodied lure with a cupped face that will move water and send out strong vibrations.

- When I'm casting over drop-offs, shoals, sunken weed beds, and other cover in deeper water, I like big, low-riding bugs with tails made from marabou or rabbit strips and Krystal Flash or Flashabou to flutter and pulsate and glitter under the surface while the cork or deerhair body chugs along on top.

- When all else is equal, I prefer smaller (size 2) bugs in natural colors (gray, white, tan) for smallmouths, and bigger (size 2/0) in combinations of white, yellow, green, and red for largemouths. On dark days and at twilight, I go with darker colors. For nighttime bugging, I like all-black, which presents a sharp silhouette to a bass looking up at it, with a white face for my own eyes. I doubt if size and color actually make much of a difference for either species, but when the fishing is slow, this is how I think.

I'm confident that I could just stick a few Tap's Bugs into my hat brim and shove a spool of tippet and a pair of needle-nose pliers into my pocket and have everything I'll need for a successful day's fishing. But, of course, I don't do that.

For many of us, much of the allure of fly fishing comes from actually catching fish on flies we've created and tied ourselves. This is as true for bass buggers as it is for trout anglers. So our bug boxes are crammed with a variety of sizes, shapes, colors, and designs that emerged from our own imaginations. We like to experiment and create, and then we like to test our creations on the water.

Bass, as we've seen, make wonderfully sympathetic judges. They eat anything that moves—an unpainted wine cork, a slab of fish skin, a bundle of feathers, a strip of leather, a glob of hair, and any concoction of ingredients whatsoever that even the most unskilled or frivolous fly tier can create. Those old-time bob fishermen caught plenty of bass, and some bug fishermen still consider the outrageous Powder Puff—which is a bristly ball of spun-and-untrimmed deerhair—a legitimate bass fly. I have no doubt that if you cast a Powder Puff upon the water, sooner or later a bass will eat it.

If you like to invent flies, I guarantee that no matter how outlandish your creation, if you keep it on the end of your line long enough, your bass bug *will* catch fish. Just don't feel smug.

When we analyze the qualities of a good bass bug, we must look beyond the baseline question, "Will it catch bass?" We already know the answer to that one.

Here, in their order of importance, are what I consider to be the characteristics of an effective bass bug:

- **Aerodynamics.** A good bass bug is light and streamlined. It offers little air resistance when you cast it. It does not twist the leader or plane or flutter off target. You should be able to cast it fifty or sixty feet with a tight loop, pinpoint accuracy, and minimal false casting on a medium-weight fly rod, and you should be able to do it all day without coming down with a case of tennis elbow.

- **Noise.** Burbles and gurgles are more lifelike and, under most conditions, attract bass better than either sharp pops or no noise at all. The angler should be able to impart a variety of noises, from soft and subtle to loud and attention-grabbing, to a good bug.

- **Behavior.** The best bass bugs are never absolutely motionless. When they're twitched and retrieved, they vibrate with life. Between twitches, they quiver and shiver, shudder and flutter.

- **Touchdown.** The way a bug falls upon the water will either attract or frighten any bass in the area, particularly if you've read the water accurately, executed a pinpoint cast, and dropped your bug onto his nose. A natural bass prey hits the water with a muffled plop or splat. Bass bugs should, too.

- **Feel.** All fish feel with their mouths, but the bass's mouth is especially sensitive. If a bass takes something into his mouth that doesn't feel right, he'll eject it so fast that you'd swear he struck short. Bass hit anything that looks edible. But only if it feels alive and edible will they hold it in their mouths long enough for the fisherman to react and set the hook.

- **Floatability.** Bass bugs are supposed to float. If they absorb water and begin sinking after a few casts, they are inefficient regardless of their other qualities. In general, a bug that rides low in the water with its belly submerged offers the bass a more natural profile, emits more lifelike, fish-attracting noises, and creates more enticing wiggles and twitches than a high rider that floats entirely atop the surface.

- **Hook.** The gape ("bite") of the hook should be wide relative to the size of the bug for consistent hookups. The point should be sharp. Barbless hooks not only penetrate better than those with barbs, but they also enable you to unhook and release your fish—not to mention yourself or your partner, should you have a casting accident—quickly and harmlessly.

- **Size.** In general, the ancient wisdom that largemouths prefer bigger bugs than smallmouths seems to hold true. But when the fish are uncooperative and the water is flat calm, I have often found that small—even panfish-sized—bugs entice more strikes from both species. On riffled water, an outsized bug usually draws more attention.

  Art Scheck, editor of *Fly Tyer* and *American Angler* magazines and bug maker extraordinaire, offers an interesting argument for small bugs: "I do know that a bass can miss a bug, particularly a big one. Maybe it has something to do with the ways that bass attack prey. When it takes a small bug, a bass generally eases up under the popper and just sucks it in like a trout taking an emerger. Most of the bass I catch on my little bugs make no more disturbance (or even less) than a bluegill does. But a bass charges larger prey. Maybe the fish throws up enough of a bow wave to push the bug away. Or perhaps the bass wants not to inhale a big bug on the first charge, but rather to stun or kill it. I've seen largemouths and smallmouths do that with minnows—chomp them as a cat bites a mouse, then let the baitfish go, then chomp it again, and then eat it. Maybe it's the fishy equivalent of tenderizing a steak. Who knows?"

  One of the intriguing mysteries of bass bugging is that its addicts hold strong—and often conflicting—opinions. Nick Lyons, for example, has written appealingly about the effectiveness and fun of casting big, bulky deerhair bugs with saltwater-weight fly rods, while Art Scheck favors small cork and balsa bugs on trout rods. "I'm not a disciple of the big-fly/big-fish school," Scheck says, "and I won't fish with anything that's a pain in the ass to cast. I've *never* caught a bass on a size 1 or larger fly, though I tried for years."

Scheck is in a distinct minority. Oh, I have caught the odd three-pound largemouth while casting little bugs for bluegills, and I do believe there are conditions and types of water where smallish bugs work better. But the "big flies for big fish" formula generally applies to predatory fish such as bass, especially largemouths.

Nick Lyons likes to use a four-legged monstrosity the size of a full-grown finch that casts best on a 10-weight saltwater outfit. "I really think," he says, "that the largest bass will come to the largest bugs, especially at dusk, at night, and particularly before there's any light on the water in the very early morning."

One of Tom Nixon's favorite bass flies is a spun-deerhair bug tied on a 7/0 hook. These bugs, he writes, are "almost impossible to make, hellish things to cast, and just about as ugly a lure as ever departed a fly tyer's vise. They have one redeeming feature—they will catch big fish."

I generally compromise between the extremes with mid-sized bugs that glug and burble and look bigger to fish than they actually are, and that I can cast comfortably on a 7- or 8-weight outfit.

- **Shape and color.** These are the features generally touted in catalogs—and in much bass-bugging literature—to distinguish one bug from another. Catalogs assume their readers have a trout-fishing, hatch-matching mentality. Catalogs tend to emphasize imitation, and they imply that you need the "right" bug—the one that imitates what the bass are looking for at that moment—to catch them. So commercial bugs are shaped, colored, and named for the prey they theoretically represent—diving frog, wounded minnow, fluttering moth, and so forth. On the water where it counts, however, color or shape—or even both of these factors taken together—are less significant than any one of those qualities listed above.

  The shape of a bug needn't imitate anything. Overall shape matters mainly because it affects how well the bug casts and how it behaves on the water. Will Ryan, author of the indispensable *Smallmouth Strategies for the Fly Rod*, prefers long cylindrical bugs for use over shoals and drop-offs, and stubby bugs for close to shore. He theorizes that skinny bugs suggest baitfish, which open-water bass are accustomed to chasing, while blunt-shaped bugs remind bass of shoreline prey such as frogs. Whether he's right or not, it's a theory that gives him confidence when he's deciding what to tie on.

  My strategy on color is to use a bug I can see on the water, because I haven't noticed that the bass give a hoot. They see only the belly of a floating bug. Everything above the water's surface is a blurry silhouette from the bass's perspective.

Many experts, naturally, disagree. Joe Brooks, for example, knew exactly what he liked: "East, North, South, West—it's all the same. Yellow is by far the best color." Charles F. Waterman, on the other hand, has suggested that he prefers white. It's no coincidence that yellow and white are easy for the fishermen to see.

- **Durability.** Bass are toothless creatures, so a good bug should survive dozens of chomps. If your bug frays, comes unraveled, or falls apart after a few fish have glommed onto it, it was poorly made. If you encounter toothy fish such as pike and pickerel (which smash bass bugs with heart-stopping enthusiasm), all bets are off.

- **Weedlessness.** A bug that slithers around, over, and through weeds and snags allows the fisherman to cast closer to the places where bass lurk. Generally speaking, however, the more effective the weedguard, the more strikes you'll miss. It's a balancing act. Under most conditions, I use bugs without weedguards and take my chances.

- **Imitativeness.** Underwater flies and lures that resemble specific prey—common species of baitfish and crayfish in particular—arguably work better than generic, suggestive lures. In my experience, at least, the opposite is actually true of topwater bass bugs. Will Ryan, in fact, sometimes likes to show the fish something dramatically different from the prevalent species of bass prey, on the theory that it will get their attention quicker than a bug or lure that looks like everything else in the water.

- **Ease/fun of tying/constructing.** If you buy your bugs, this criterion is irrelevant. But if you're into creating your own bugs, you'll probably rank it near the top. As Art Scheck says, "Right now, I'm having a lot of fun painting corks and bits of wood, and so I'm fishing mostly hard-bodied bugs. Five years hence, things might be different."

By these standards, spun deerhair bugs seem to offer many advantages over their balsa and cork counterparts, and few disadvantages, although the practitioners sometimes disagree vigorously.

- The biggest difference between deerhair and hard-bodied bugs is how they feel in a bass's mouth. According to Dave Whitlock, "A bass has an amazing sensitivity to touch on its body and mouth, much greater than that of a trout or char. This means: use flies that have soft, realistic textures. . . . A bass bug made of clipped deer hair will nearly always be held in a bass's mouth *two or three times* longer than a hard plastic or wooden fly or lure of the same size and shape. In fact, bass can inhale and exhale a hard fly or lure so fast it's easy to think they actually missed it. I've often observed this faster-than-a-blink reaction when testing new fly designs on bass I keep in large aquariums and ponds."

Art Scheck, who holds strong minority opinions on many subjects, offers a provocative dissent. "Conventional wisdom," he writes in a personal letter, "says that bass eject hard bugs quickly, or at least more quickly than they spit out deerhair or soft-foam bugs. I simply haven't found that to be so. The night before last, I caught (in a manner of speaking) a smallmouth that ate a little balsa popper while I was wading along the shoreline and not paying attention. My bug was sitting on the water about twenty feet away, at the end of about thirty feet of slack line. I never heard the fish take the fly, and had no idea I'd caught it until I stripped in the slack. Such things have happened to me more than once.

"I'm not sure how much softness and texture matter to a bass. I suspect very little or not at all. All flies, after all, contain hard hooks. And fish eat all sorts of things that are hard or spiny. We have a pet bass in the office. When it eats a crawdad, it sucks the critter into its throat and mashes the hell out of it for a while. Then it blows out the claws. Obviously, the bass feels something in its throat. But I can't imagine it has sensation at all akin to ours. . . . I've seen lots of bass eat hard poppers and hang on to them until it occurred to me that setting the hook might be a good idea."

This has happened to me countless times: I drop my deer-hair bug into a hole in the lily pads or alongside some downed timber, and then I shift my attention to a heron stalking the shallows or an osprey cruising overhead, or I decide to refill my coffee mug, or light my pipe, or button my shirt, or laugh at my partner's shaggy-dog story. When I look back for my bug, it's disappeared. The expanding rings on the water tell me that a bass devoured it when I wasn't looking. Belatedly, I tighten my line . . . and he's still there, happily chomping on what, to him, feels like something good to eat. Perhaps he would have done the same had my bug been made of cork or balsa. But deerhair gives me more confidence.

Although not all bass behave identically, bless 'em, you need quick reflexes to hook bass consistently on hard-bodied lures. With deerhair bugs, it's actually best to pause for a count of three to allow the fish to close his mouth and turn away before you set the hook.

Decision: For feel—deerhair.

- You can decorate hard bugs with feathers that breathe and rubber legs that vibrate on the water to enhance their action. But you are still left with that hard, unnatural body. As Nick Lyons has written, "The soft fly can be manipulated with so much more subtlety than a hard lure—it can be stopped dead, flirted, fluttered, eased, and swum in any direction—it can actually be more effective than other lures, more alive than the hardbodied plug or spoon."

  Decision: Deerhair bugs produce more alluring action.

- The heavier and denser the material, the harder it will hit the water and the more likely it will spook rather than attract a bass. A skillful caster, of course, can make any bug land any way he wants, but deerhair bugs are more forgiving. It's hard *not* to make them fall onto the water with an enticing splat or plop.

  Art Scheck, defending hard-bodied bugs again, says: "The other beef about cork and balsa bugs is that they land too hard and can scare a bass in the neighborhood. That might be true if we were to compare extremes. A big, rubber-legged cork bug built on a heavy-wire popper hook hits the water with quite a splash, while your dad's deerhair bug lands almost as gently as a dry fly. But one of my balsa bugs made on a size 4 Aberdeen hook lands more gently than most store-bought deerhair bugs equipped with rubber legs and molded plastic eyes. Besides, just as it is in trout fishing, 99 percent of delicacy comes from the hand of the angler. I've dropped a lot of cork bugs right on the noses of largemouths, and the bass just tipped up and sucked 'em in. Every time that has happened, however, I had made a good cast (I'm allowed ten a year, by contract) with a smallish popper."

  Decision: Deerhair bugs plop onto the water more naturally than hard-bodied bugs of the same size.

- Commercial hard-bodied bugs are designed to make a single kind of noise. They pop, push water, or slide. Low-riding, porous deerhair bugs, on the other hand, can be manipulated to give you whatever you want: that delicious bass-attracting glug and gurgle, a quiet, bubbly slither, or an attention-getting ker-PLOOP. If you want a POP that will wake up a distant bass, a hard tug on a big flat-nosed deerhair bug will create a noise almost as loud as a cup-faced cork popper.

Decision: A single deerhair bug can be manipulated to produce a variety of enticing noises. Hard-bodied bugs don't burble or glug.

- Hard bugs, of course, float forever. Some skeptics claim that deerhair bugs soak up water and float poorly after they've been on the water for a while and have caught a bass or two. However, if the deerhair is tightly packed on the hook before it's trimmed, and if you work plenty of flotant into it when it's still dry, it takes a long time for the bug to become waterlogged. When it does, you can simply squeeze the water out of it.

  In fact, I *want* my deerhair bugs to absorb a little water. I want them to ride awash in, not high on, the water's surface. Low riders glug and burble better, and they mimic the way natural prey appears to bass. For that reason, when I apply flotant to an all-deerhair bug, I leave the underside untreated so it will soak up a little water and ride lower. I do, however, saturate the deerhair head of a Deacon, which tends to ride low in the water anyway.

Decision: Hard-bodied bugs float higher and longer, but for more versatile floatability, the edge goes to deerhair.

- The bodies of hard bugs are unquestionably durable. But the body of a well-made deerhair bug will stand up to thousands of casts and dozens of bass chomps. Generally, it's the tail, wings, or legs of any bug—hard- or soft-bodied—that go first.

Decision: Hard-bodied bugs are more durable, but only by a nose.

- The castability and weedlessness of both hard-bodied and deerhair bugs are limited only by their creator's imagination. There are many ways to affix effective weedguards to both deerhair and hard bugs, and small, streamlined bugs of all materials can be cast comfortably and accurately with a properly balanced outfit.

Decision: Dead heat for both criteria.

- Hard-bodied bugs can be shaped and painted and decked out with natural and synthetic appendages so that they are virtually precise imitations of actual bass prey. With some exceptions—Joe Messinger's clever (and very difficult-to-tie) Hair Frog, for example—the inherent limitations of deerhair produces bugs that are more suggestive than imitative.

Decision: When it comes to precise imitation of natural bass prey, hard-bodied bugs win by several lengths. But it hardly matters.

- Fly tiers enjoy spinning and clipping deerhair. Model builders like to assemble, glue, shape, and paint balsa, cork, and other hard materials. Both methods of construction can be fussy and, at times, frustrating. But neither requires artistry or unusual talent.

  Decision: Whatever turns you on.

In the final analysis, both hard and soft bugs are proven bass catchers, and regardless of what you choose to tie to your leader, it's your ability to pick likely targets, cast accurately, and manipulate the bug convincingly that will draw strikes.

Bass on Top

"There is a prevalent notion that the small-mouth bass is the 'game' species *par excellence.* In common with most anglers I at one time shared this belief but from a long series of observations I am of the opinion that the large-mouth bass, all things being equal, displays as much pluck, and exhibits as untiring fighting qualities as its small-mouth cousin."
    James A. Henshall, *Book of the Black Bass* (1881)

"I have never understood bass as I think I understand trout. . . . I just can't figure them out."
    Harold F. Blaisdell, *The Philosophical Fisherman* (1969)

"If I sound vague on these matters it's on purpose—for I lack the conviction of some anglers who will tell you exactly when to fish."
    Charles F. Waterman, *Fly Rodding for Bass* (1989)

Smallmouth and largemouth bass, collectively called "black bass," are closely related members of the *Micropterus* genus. In temperament, appetite, lifestyle, and behavior, their similarities far outweigh their differences, and for most practical angling purposes, and particularly for the bass-bug fisherman, it's generally appropriate to think about them as if they were identical. "Both species," writes Henshall, "are remarkably active, muscular and voracious, with large, hard and tough mouths; are very bold in biting, and when hooked exhibit gameness and endurance second to no other fish." For our purposes, both species are equally susceptible to a well-twitched bass bug. The word "bass" does the job for both.

Smallmouths and largemouths, of course, are not taxonomically identical. For one thing, largemouths, um, have larger mouths. Henshall quotes a poem by Fred Mather (who will never be confused with Robert Frost) to explicate some ways to distinguish one from the other:

> The little mouth has little scales
> There's red in his handsome eye;
> The scales extend on his vertical fins,
> And his forehead is round and high.
>
> His forehead is full and high, my boys,
> And he sleeps the winter through;
> He likes the rocks in summer time,
> *Micropterus dolomieu.*
>
> The big-mouth has the biggest scales,
> And a pit scooped in his head;
> His mouth is cut beyond his eye,
> In which is nary a red.
>
> In his eye is nary a red, my boys,
> But keen and well he sees;
> He has a dark stripe on his side,
> *Micropterus salmonides.*

Smallmouths are thought of as northern fish—though there are great smallmouth lakes in the South. They are associated with deep, rocky lakes and cold, clear rivers. Largemouths, which are native to the southern states, thrive in warm, weedy, shallow ponds, impoundments, and backwaters—though there are excellent largemouth lakes in New England and the northern Midwest and West. These generalizations work up to a point, perhaps because smallmouths spawn most successfully on gravelly bottoms, while largemouths do just fine on mud and silt.

In fact, however, the cousins are remarkably adaptable. They often inhabit the same water. In lakes that hold both largemouths and smallmouths, each will lay claim to a different territory—the smallmouths around rocky shoals and boulder-strewn shorelines near drop-offs into deeper water, and the largemouths in shallow, weedy mud-bottomed coves. On several occasions, however, I have taken one of each species from alongside the same fallen tree or boat dock on consecutive casts. After more than a century of migration and transplanting, the territories of both species range over most of North America and overlap considerably.

Their differing preferences for types of water, especially the bottom, probably account for the somewhat different preferences the two species exhibit for prey. If smallmouths seem to like crayfish better than largemouths do, for example, it's because crayfish favor the same cold, gravel-bottomed waters that the fish do. And largemouths are associated with frogs because frogs like the same kind of water. But both species of bass are confirmed omnivores and will devour crayfish and frogs with equal voracity whenever they can find them.

The single most important variable in the location, movement, and activity of all cold-blooded creatures is the temperature of their environment. The body temperature of all fish rises and falls along with the temperature of the water around them. They lapse into a semi-comatose state when the temperature rises significantly above or falls much below their comfort range. On the outer extremes of comfortable temperatures, they feed little. In a body of water, or at a time of year, where the water temperature varies in different areas, fish will seek the most comfortable water.

When the water temperature is ideal, bass feel terrific and feed most actively.

For the bass-bug fisherman, the key to finding and catching bass is understanding how to locate water where the fish feel terrific.

Largemouths and smallmouths both tolerate a wide range of water temperatures. They can survive in waters from the mid-30's to 90°, although they like it best when the temperature ranges between 60° and 75° for at least six months of the year. When it drops below 55°, the metabolisms of both species slow down. Their appetites grow dull, and they are unlikely to hit bass bugs on the surface. Smallmouths prefer somewhat cooler temperatures—55°–75° is ideal—whereas largemouths are most active when the water's between 60° and 80°. Interestingly, however, smallmouths stop feeding almost entirely when the water temperature drops below 50°, while largemouths feed sporadically even at the coldest extremes. Unlike smallmouths, largemouths are often taken by ice fishermen.

The temperature of shallow water is probably the single most important key to success for the bug fisherman. When bass find the shallows too cold or too warm, they seek comfort in deep water, where it's harder to entice them to the surface. Generally speaking, both species of bass move to the warm shallows in the springtime, migrate into deeper water in the midday heat of summer, and return to the shallows as the water cools toward autumn. Then as winter approaches and the shallow water grows uncomfortably cold, they return to the depths to sulk.

Those times when bass swarm along the shoreline are, of course, prime for bugging. But there are plenty of excellent topwater opportunities even in the worst heat of summer. Largemouths thrive year-round in weedy, shallow-water eutrophic ponds and slow-moving rivers, and smallmouths find comfort in cool, shallow, oxygen-rich streams. Additionally, short-term variables such as time of day, weather, wind, and sun keep bass on the move constantly. Except for winter, there are times throughout the year when you can catch bass on topwater bugs.

The old aphorism is a good guide: The most pleasant time of day for the bass-bug angler to be outdoors is also the best time to catch fish.

- On the margins of the season—early in the spring and late in the fall—bass seek comfort in sheltered, sun-warmed shallows in the middle of the day, when it's also the most pleasant for the fisherman to be on the water.

- During the dog days of summer, bass gravitate to the relative comfort of cool water. They sulk in heavy shade or deep water when the sun is high, then prowl the shallows to feed in the cool of late afternoon, evening, after dark, and early morning. A few days of soft, refreshing summer rain, or even a heavy cloud cover, might keep them actively prowling the shallows all day. The weather conditions and times of day when shallow water is coolest—those peaceful, magical times for the angler—are when you will find bass foraging in bugging water.

- In the temperate months when you want to be outdoors all the time—late spring and early autumn—bass are active all day long in bright as well as shaded shallow water.

- Late fall, winter, and early spring are uncomfortable times for both bass and bass anglers. Bug fishermen are well advised to take their cue from the fish and hunker down in a warm place.

Bass, like all organisms, are preoccupied with three powerful survival instincts: to eat, to avoid being eaten, and to procreate. Their behaviors derive from their instincts to survive as individuals and as a species.

In its season, the spawning drive overrides all other concerns. Bass shed a good deal of their normal wariness in their preoccupation with building and protecting their nests. They feed less, but they become correspondingly more belligerent and attack all invaders of their territory with mindless hostility.

Some fishermen claim to find bass harder to catch when they're spawning. I have found the opposite to be the case, especially with smallmouths. Every bass in the water migrates to the shallows, so they're easy to find. They're also easy to attract. A bug churning up a fuss over their heads screams "Enemy!" and makes bass—especially the males—see red.

The spawning impulse seizes bass when the water temperature approaches 60°—February or March in the South, and as late as early

July in the northern extremes of their range. The fisherman can pin-point spawning time on any body of water either by using a thermometer or simply by looking for the distinctive round, sand-colored beds in water from two to eight feet deep. Drop a bug atop one of those beds and you're almost guaranteed an angry strike.

Male bass do most of the housekeeping work. They move to the shallows to build their nests while the roe-heavy females linger along the edges of deeper water. After the females have dropped in, laid their eggs, and departed, the males remain behind—first to guard the nests, then eventually to attack and disperse their young. Most of the bass you'll catch on bugs during spawning time will be the smaller, more aggressive males.

Some anglers refuse to fish when bass are on their spawning beds on the grounds that the fish are too easy to catch and should not, in any case, be disturbed during this all-absorbing process. If you want to protect and conserve the fish, they claim, taking them off their beds is unethical.

Work all shaded shorelines carefully.

I take a more straightforward and practical approach. Some of my fastest and most memorable topwater bass-bug action has come during spawning time. Sometimes this is not particularly challenging fishing—but sometimes I don't need a challenge to have fun. I catch relatively few of those fat, precious females. I use barbless hooks, fight the fish aggressively, land them quickly, release them unharmed, and return them near the spot where I hooked them. I have caught what I suppose to be the same feisty male bass from the same nest on consecutive days often enough to be convinced that he simply returned to his post and resumed his duty after being hooked, none the worse or wiser for the interruption.

The period immediately preceding spawning time finds bass foraging in the shallows after their long winter of semihibernation. Once the water temperature hits about 55°, bass begin feeding heavily to build up their strength for spawning. They prowl the warm shoreline water where their prey, as well as they themselves, are most comfortable, and they gobble bass bugs because they're hungry. The same ethics that censor fishing during the spawn should even more logically keep fishermen off the water during the prespawn, when females are on the move and as easy to catch as the males, but I have never heard this argument.

The postspawn period, which lasts a few weeks after the fry disperse and adult bass abandon their beds, finds them less interested than normal in eating. Fortunately for the fishermen (and fortunate, too, for the survival of their species), not all bass in any given body of water operate on the identical schedule. Some individuals start and complete their spawning earlier than others, and some recover faster than others. Even during the postspawn period, the fisherman can always find bass that are willing to take a bug.

As late spring moves into summer, bass resume heavy feeding, and they don't stop until winter drops the water temperature below their comfort level.

Anyone who fishes for them regularly has noticed that sometimes summer bass are hungry and active, while at other times they seem lockjawed. Figuring out when and where to fish is especially challenging during the long summer season.

Fish when you can, of course. Going fishing is always better than the alternatives. But if you have a choice, go when the conditions are most favorable. In the absence of hard data, I respond to the "feel" of the day. I prefer what I think of as "soft" conditions. Any humid, dark, and still summer day beckons me to the water. Usually, the margins of the day—early morning around daybreak, and again in the evening— feel "soft." These are the times when the sun does not blaze upon the

Overcast sky and flat water: a "soft" day.

water, when the wind has not yet come up, or after it has died down. If a quiet mist is falling, so much the better.

These are the times when the entire pond seems alive and vital—when bullfrogs grump and grumble, when swallows and bats swoop overhead, when insects buzz and dart and pepper the water, when you can hear the ker-SLOSH of a feeding bass in the next cove. These are also the times when water-skiers, speedboaters, and swimmers—and other fishermen—are not likely to interrupt the stillness of your pond.

I suppose I've acquired this "feel" for soft summer days by having fished obsessively for half a century under every conceivable condition, so that I've internalized the variables that my subconscious associates with fast bass bugging. But it bears up under analysis:

- Bass can see and hear a bug on the surface more easily when the water is flat than when it's choppy. Wind from some quarters—no doubt because it's associated with the movement of weather fronts and the changes in barometric pressure and relative humidity that accompany them—makes for better fishing than others. The old poem is still a good guideline:

> When the wind is from the east,
> That's when fish bite the least.
> When the wind is from the north,
> That's when fishermen go not forth.
> When the wind is from the west,
> That's when fish bite the best.
> And when the wind is from the south,
> It blows the bait to the fish's mouth.

To that I would append my own final, awkward couplet:

> When there's not a breath of breeze,
> You'll catch a hundred bass with ease.

- In the summer, bass find shaded water cooler and more comfortable than sun-drenched water. Overhanging shoreline bushes, weed beds, fallen trees, docks, and other sources of shade also protect them from overhead predators, which can spot them less easily in the shade—or anywhere if it's overcast or drizzling.

- Bass are particularly uncomfortable when bright sun is accompanied by low relative humidity. Cliff Hauptman, in his important book *The Fly Fisher's Guide to Warmwater Lakes,* attributes this to the bass's aversion to ultraviolet rays—*not* to light itself. Rain, cloud cover, and even just high relative humidity filter out this source of discomfort, and under these conditions, bass will not retreat to deep water or dark shade as they tend to on a bright, dry day. The absence of strong ultraviolet rays explains why dawn and dusk, when the sun does not beat down on the water, are prime bass-bugging times. But Hauptman points out that midday fishing—when bass see best—can offer excellent fishing, provided that the UV factor is low. In fact, he notes that expert basser Doug Hannon, who keeps detailed records, catches most of his big fish between 10:00 A.M. and 3:00 P.M. Hannon, of course, does much of his fishing subsurface.

- Bass, like all shallow-water fish, are extremely sensitive to barometric pressure. They become active on a falling barometer and grow uncomfortable when high-pressure systems prevail. Fishing can be slow for the first day or two after a cold front moves through, but bass feed aggressively when a storm is approaching. Fish cannot sense barometric pressure below ten feet of water, but they are sensitive to this variable in the shallows, where we hunt them with bugs. In high-pressure conditions, they leave prime bass-bugging shallows and migrate to deeper, more comfortable water.

- Bass feed actively at night, especially during the summer's hottest months. Knowing they can't be seen, bass shed their fear of predators in the dark and roam the shallows boldly. Night fishing is probably the bug fisherman's best chance to catch a truly large bass. Those old survivors are never stupid, but they do tend to lose some of their inhibitions after dark. They hunt more by sound than sight, so a big, noisy black bug will attract them. I know many fishermen who say they've tried night fishing for bass in the summer and have found it disappointing. I suspect they've become discouraged and quit too early. There typically comes a lull in bass activity in the first hour or two after nightfall, and then—around ten o'clock on my New England ponds—the fish seem to become acclimated to the darkness and start foraging—and they will forage until dawn. For some reason, they seem to hit better on dark than on moonlit nights.

When I began feeling crowded on my favorite bugging waters, I quit fly fishing for bass altogether for a while and became a trout specialist. Ironically, it was an afternoon of trout fishing that brought me back to bugging for bass.

The local brook with the Indian name—my "home" trout stream—flows low and warm and sluggish in the summer, and I usually stopped fishing there when the first hot spell arrived in June. But then a three-day July gullywasher brought the water level up nearly a foot. It was running pretty clear, though. From my observation post at the bridge rail, it looked like a trout stream again, and I couldn't resist the quixotic urge to give it a try.

I retrieved my seven-foot fiberglass car rod from the trunk, tied a fat Muddler to the tippet, pulled on my hip boots, and slithered down the muddy slope. The currents swirled and eddied around the boulders just the way they did in May when hatchery browns and brookies sipped Hendrickson spinners.

The brook trout, of course, had all turned belly-up by now, and as relatively hardy as they are, I doubted that any of the browns had survived the June drought, either.

Well, maybe one brown had made it. That's all I wanted.

I figured it was all pretend. But it was good to stand in my stream again with the little 4-weight rod in my hand and the soft rain on my face, waking that Muddler across the currents, and I quickly lost myself in the rhythms and memories of it.

The strike came hard and sudden and unexpected, a strong boiling swirl that engulfed that Muddler, and when I raised my rod and felt the muscular pull at the other end, I thought: Yes! Big carryover brown. I'm a genius.

Then my brown trout jumped, and it wasn't a brown. It wasn't any kind of trout. It was a largemouth bass. About a three-pounder.

Nuts, I thought. A damn bass. Some genius.

He jumped again, rattling his gills, and when he hit the water he sent waves sloshing against both banks of the narrow pool. Then he surged downstream, heading for the tailout. I gave him as much pressure as I dared. I feared for my 3X tippet. The little rod bent double.

It felt familiar, and I realized how much I'd missed bass bugging. I'd missed it a lot.

By the time I managed to turn that bass and work him to my feet and pinch his lower lip between my thumb and forefinger and lift him from the water, I was thinking: Maybe I *am* a genius.

After I released him, I sat on a boulder to ponder it. My little trout stream meanders through swamp and marsh and woods, parallels the railroad tracks behind the strip mall, and passes under several highway bridges. A few smaller streams join it along the way before it finally empties into one of my formerly "secret" bass ponds, a place I quit fishing when I realized it was no longer a secret.

I doubted that my bass had retreated up into the stream to escape attacking spinnerbaits. He had simply wandered away, searching for food and shelter and comfort, the way all fish do. To the bass, the little stream was part of his pond.

Where one bass lived, I figured, there likely would be others. Best of all, no bass boat could navigate this brook.

And so I began exploring my stream, and then other trout-sized streams, for summer bass. I studied topographic maps, looking for thin blue lines that connected, however indirectly, to known bass waters. I trekked through bogs and woods to check them out. Many of them proved to be dried-up streambeds or otherwise fishless. No prospector strikes gold with every swing of his pickax.

But enough of them held bass to revive my lust for bass fishing with the fly rod. I fished those little streams trout-style—drifting bugs and bushy dry flies against the banks and twitching them across the currents.

And I widened my search. I hunted down waters that held bass—
and were inaccessible to bass boats. I found enough bassy places to
keep me happy—and solitary.

And so I became a born-again bass-bug fanatic.

If the best *time* to go fishing is *when* you can, then the best *place* to
fish is *where* you can. But just as some conditions increase the likeli-
hood of finding fast fishing, so, too, do some bodies of water—and
some places on those waters—offer better chances than others.

Finding good bass water depends on your definition of "good." My
ideal bass water meets all of these criteria:

- It's nearby, which allows me to go on the spur of the moment
  without a lot of planning and fussing.

- It holds a reasonably large population of bass, including enough
  big ones to give me the realistic hope of catching a trophy.

- It's easy for an angler to fish from shore or launch a canoe or
  float tube there, but it provides no direct road access or concrete boat ramp for trailered bass boats.

- It's small and intimate enough that I can walk or paddle from
  one end to the other in an hour or two and hit all my favorite
  hot spots in a single trip.

- It features some combination of steep, brushy banks, weeds,
  fallen timber, dark coves, and rocky points, with plenty of
  shaded shoreline cover to attract and hold bass and provide
  interesting bug-casting targets.

- It's my secret, and I share it only with my friends.

Since I chose not to compete with the bass boats on most of my
favorite old local bass waters, I've followed rumors, hunches, and
topographic maps to dozens of new places. Many of them meet several
of my criteria, and a few are close to ideal. I've found healthy popula-
tions of both largemouths and smallmouths in trout-sized streams and
brooks that flow into and out of known bass lakes, in farm ponds
and millponds, in golf-course water hazards, in quarry pits, and even in
the tiny reservoirs that rural villagers used to dig to hold emergency
fire-fighting water. In fact, I've found few bodies of water that *don't*
harbor bass.

Many parts of the country are speckled with tank ponds, canals,
irrigation ponds and ditches, duck ponds, and lagoons. Sooner or later,
bass seem to appear in almost all man-made bodies of water, even
those built for decoration or recreation in housing developments or

This pond once served as a reservoir for a local fire department.

A hidden woodland bass pond—no house, no boat ramps.

industrial parks. I've been able to slide my canoe onto many private ponds that offer no public access simply by asking permission—and these waters are often lightly fished.

Bass do not distribute themselves evenly throughout any lake, pond, or river. On the contrary, they congregate in areas that meet their needs for comfort, food, and protection from predators. Small waters are easier to "read" than big lakes or reservoirs—and if you're "illiterate," you can prospect their shorelines blindly until you find fish.

The best way to fish bass bugs is to paddle along parallel to a shoreline and cast toward the bank. A good bass shoreline offers one likely bass hideout after another—the dark cave under an overhanging hemlock, the trunk of a fallen old oak, an alley in the reeds, a pothole in a bed of lily pads, a jumble of boulders—and much of the mesmerizing allure of bass bugging comes from paddling slowly, combing that shoreline, and hitting the bull's-eye of each of those bassy targets as it comes along. As A. J. McClane has written, "Most bass bugging is done in close to shore among rocks, weed patches, and fallen timber. To me, this is the most interesting way of fishing for bass."

Bass congregate around what has come to be called "structure." Structure and cover are not always the same. Cover—weed beds,

A deliciously "bassy" cove.

Fallen trees, weed beds, and shade from overhanging vegetation make a perfect hiding place for bass.

fallen trees, overhanging bushes, boat docks—hides bass. Structure can be any kind of underwater object—a stump, rock, piling, or bridge abutment as well as that fallen tree—or it might be a hump, depression, trough, or drop-off on the bottom. Bass like to lurk alongside, under, and over structure, especially when it's near cover. Sonar helps the tournament pros identify subsurface structure, and it would probably help the bass-bug angler, too. But shoreline bugging normally requires only the ability to recognize the obvious, because most shallow-water structure is visible.

You'll often find bass scattered in what appears to be a random way along any shoreline. If you knew what was beneath the surface—a depression on the bottom, a waterlogged tree branch, a jumble of rocks, a patch of submerged weeds, even an old truck tire—you'd understand that the fish's location wasn't really random at all. By the same token, places that look good to you sometimes come up empty, probably because what's beneath the surface lacks what the bass need.

In really good bass water, you might actually find more attractive bass-holding targets than there are bass. You'll also come to appreciate the fact that bass, like people, can be fickle and unpredictable. Nothing is certain in bass-bug fishing.

For example, Will Ryan tells me he's having fun catching small-mouths on bugs over deep, open water. The key, says Ryan, is finding clear, reasonably flat water, so that the fish can hear the bug and then locate it visually. He prefers big, noisy poppers that kick up a signifi-cant fuss. He casts over shoals and sunken boulders, burbles his bug along steadily, and he brings up bass from as deep as fifteen feet in water that most bass fisherman would drag with heavy jigs and full-sinking lines.

Whether you stick to the shoreline or explore open water, you'll consistently catch more and bigger bass if you aim your bug for *edges*, those places where two or more types of holding water rub against each other. Edges enable bass to lurk in more than one environment at the same time.

A brushy shore.

More than undifferentiated cover, edges give bass everything they're looking for: protection from predators, comfortable water temperatures, and abundant forage. Typically, a bass will hide under something—a fallen tree, a weed bed, an overhanging bush, or a boat dock that protects him from the sun and hides him from predators—and keep a lookout on the open sunlit water that abuts his cover, where baitfish or other bass food might appear. He'll dart out from the one environment to snag a meal—or a bass bug—from the other.

Places where several edges meet make prime bass cover. The more edges that converge in a single spot, offering both cover and structure, the better. That's the place to shoot for.

Bass-bug casting is target shooting. Every cast should have a purpose and a bull's-eye. Purposeful casting is at least half the fun of bugging for bass. If you aim for edges—and hit them consistently—you'll catch more and bigger bass.

Topwater edges provide clues to what's under the water. Here are some types of visible edges that the bass-bug fisherman should look for and shoot at:

- **The line where any two environments meet,** such as sunlight and shade, riffled and calm water, dark and light bottom, shallow and deep water, open and clogged water, clear and

Mixed shoreline weed beds.

murky water, moving and still water (such as where a stream empties into a pond), cool and warm water (such as a spring-hole), and two different species of weeds.

- **Weed beds.** Although bass will scatter themselves underneath any significant patch of floating weeds, more of them will usually lurk along its edges. Lily pads, for example, provide excellent shelter from the sun and from predators. The edges of any weed bed define the meeting place of several environments—sun and shade, shallow and deeper water, weedy and open water, and often two different kinds of bottom. Likewise, the visible alleys and potholes inside a weed bed signify some kind of bottom variation—a trench or hole of deep water, a rocky bottom bordering mud, an underwater boulder, or a springhole.

- **Underwater structure.** Any underwater object that sticks out of the surface makes a likely and easily identified bass-bug target. Bass orient themselves alongside boulders, reeds, stubs, pilings, bridge abutments, and, in fact, anything whatsoever that breaks up their underwater environment. The classic largemouth hangout is a big old tree that has toppled into the water and lain there for a few years. Perhaps only a few gnarled twigs poke out of the water. But if the trunk is a foot thick, it takes

A downed tree provides hiding places for bass.

little imagination to picture the jungle of waterlogged branches under the surface. Water that's deep enough to cover that big tree is bassy water indeed. Visualize the tree's underwater borders and rake the whole area thoroughly. A fallen tree creates hundreds of bass-holding edges, combinations of structure and cover that give them excellent places to hide from enemies, avoid the sun, and snipe at minnows, frogs, and terrestrial creatures. If you take a big bass from a fallen tree, don't be too quick to move along. You might catch three or four more—and bigger ones—if you fish it thoroughly and patiently.

- **The borders of the water.** Bass generally avoid the mid-depths of any body of water. They orient themselves to the surface, bottom, and shoreline. Bass-bug fishing doesn't really focus only on the surface edge. When you cast bugs to the shoreline, you are actually casting to fish that are oriented to all three

Bass are likely to be found where a steep shoreline meets large rocks and weeds.

A shallow cove with weed beds.

edges. Whenever you target some kind of structure along the shoreline, you're working one of those rich compound edges. If an otherwise likely looking shoreline does not harbor bass, the water is probably too shallow. Look for a shoreline with banks that rise almost straight up from the water. Steep banks usually betray deep-enough water against the edge to hold bass tight.

- **Bottom edges.** Study the bottom as well as the top of the water. Peer down through the surface with polarized glasses and look for places where mud meets silt, silt meets gravel, gravel meets boulder—anyplace where the color of the bottom changes. Fish any edges where submerged weed beds abut open water. Notice abrupt changes in water depth, too. Will Ryan catches smallmouths along the edges of drop-offs and shoals where the depth might change abruptly from twelve to twenty feet. He calls it "deep, open water," but he's still targeting his casts for bass-holding edges.

- **Moving water.** Bass—especially smallmouths—are sometimes found in fast-flowing rivers and streams with distinctive riffles, runs, channels, eddies, and pockets. In moving water, bass behave much like trout. They always lie facing upstream, and they normally hold a stationary position and wait for the currents to bring food to them. At the same time, they do not like to fight heavy currents. Look for them in the comfortable cushions in front of and behind boulders, toward the tail of long, slow pools, in deep channels, in the soft water against the banks, and along current seams. Under low-light conditions, river bass go on the prowl, and you'll find them foraging on the surface in big pools.

The more you understand bass habits and preferences, the better your chances will be for dropping a bug within striking distance of them. But don't lose sight of the first rule: The best time and place to go fishing is when and where you can.

Gearing Up

"Fly-fishing holds the same relation to bait-fishing that poetry does to prose; and, while each method will ever have its enthusiastic admirers, only he who can skillfully handle the comely fly-rod, and deftly cast the delicate fly, can truly and fully enjoy the aesthetics of the gentle art."
    James A. Henshall, *Book of the Black Bass* (1881)

"Two things make it possible to bug-fish with light fly tackle. One is the forward-taper line and the other is a streamlined bug."
    H. G. Tapply, *The Sportsman's Notebook* (1964)

"Fine tackle is one of the joys of any kind of fly fishing and most veterans have more than they really need. There's room for disagreement but there are basic needs."
    Charles F. Waterman, *Fly Rodding for Bass* (1989)

When I began bass-bug fishing with my dad, we used split-cane bamboo rods, silk lines, and gut leaders. The rods were heavy and soft and pretty clunky. Gut leader sections came in short lengths, and they weren't very strong for their diameter. The taper of a fly line was designated by mysterious letters—HDH, for example, signified a double-tapered line, although matching it to a rod involved guesswork and trial and error. Those silk lines needed to be dried and greased up several times in an afternoon, because silk would sink. When a day's fishing ended, we stripped our line off the reel into loose coils on a newspaper to dry or else it would rot. The coating on those old silk lines often cracked and otherwise deteriorated. If we left it on the reel over the winter, it would become kinky and tacky and useless. I was just a kid, but I knew enough to take good care of my line, because fly lines were expensive.

I doubt if I could cast a bass bug very efficiently on one of those old 1950 outfits today. But I could back then, or at least it seemed to me that I could.

When I went off fishing on my own in the days before I was old enough to drive, which I did almost every day that I didn't go off with my father, I brought along my special bicycle rod, an engineering marvel constructed from telescoping tubular steel. When it was collapsed into itself, it measured less than two feet long—ideal for gripping across the handlebars. It had a permanent set and the action of overcooked linguine. I caught a lot of bass by casting bugs with that rod.

I have emphasized that you can catch bass on almost any floating object with a hook in it. Put it on the water near a fish, give it a few twitches, and eventually some bass will try to eat it.

The same principle applies to the other components of your bass-bugging outfit. You can get a bug onto the water with any rig. With a poorly designed and unbalanced outfit, you'll be able to cast only short distances and with little accuracy, and you will find it hard, exhausting work. But if it enables you to drop a bug near a bass, he won't care.

A lot of fishermen try fly casting bass bugs and abandon it quickly because it seems too difficult and laborious. I suspect that most of those quitters start with light trout-weight outfits or with cheap, poorly matched, hand-me-down or yard-sale gear. Modern floating fly lines tapered and weighted to handle a bass bug and strung on a high-modulus graphite rod designed for that size of line make casting seem as natural as throwing a ball. With a well-balanced outfit, fly casting is intuitive and easy and fun.

Visit any fly shop or call a reputable mail-order company, ask for an 8-weight bass-bugging outfit, and you can't go wrong. You'll end up with a weight-forward (forward-tapered, or "bass-bug" tapered), 8-weight, floating line (designated WF-8-F), a rod built to cast that line, and a reel for storing the line. Nowadays, gearing up is just that easy.

Most shops will encourage you to try a rod on their casting pond or in their parking lot, and they'll be sure to put a sweet outfit in your hands. If you're a beginner, the clerk might give you a few gentle casting pointers. He'll want you to find it pleasant and easy, because then you'll be likely to make a purchase. Be sure to try it with a bass bug tied to the leader. That's the only way to tell if the outfit will serve that specific casting purpose.

You can get a complete outfit for under $200. It will do the job, and do it better than the most expensive equipment available fifty years ago. Fly-fishing gear is like most things: You get what you pay for, but you might be paying for features that are irrelevant to how well the outfit

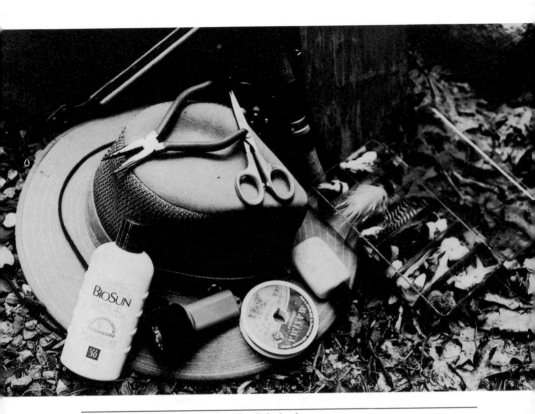

All the gear you need to fly fish for bass.

actually casts a bass bug. If you want "the best" and appreciate fine workmanship, expensive components, and eye-catching aesthetics, you can invest a lot of money in bass-bugging gear and consider it well spent.

One of the attractions of bass-bug fishing, at least for me, is its simplicity. When I go trout fishing, I wear a vest that's packed with a dozen fly boxes, several spools of tippet, spare leaders, gunk that floats flies and gunk that sinks leaders, strike indicators, containers of split shot, and a lot of other junk I don't even know is there, like old candy bars and paperback novels, along with a jangling array of doo-dads pinned and tied to it. And I always worry that I don't have what I'll need with me.

When I go bugging, I bring one box that holds a small assortment of bugs (or I just hook half a dozen into the crown of my cap), and I know I've got more flies than I'll need. I stick a pair of needle-nose pliers and a spool of tippet material into one pocket and insect repellent and sunblock into another. I slip on my sunglasses and a wide-brimmed hat, string up my rod, and I'm fully equipped.

THE LINE

The term "fly casting" is, technically, misleading. Fly casting really involves casting a line that happens to have a fly attached to the end of it. You can fly cast without a fly and scarcely notice the difference. When you select an outfit for most kinds of fly fishing, you first choose a suitable line and then select a rod that will cast that line.

Because bass bugs generally are heavy and air-resistant, smooth, easy casting calls for a line with enough density to compensate for the bulk of the bug. A 7- or 8-weight line (which, if you care, means a line of which the first thirty feet weighs anywhere from 177 to 218 grains) will handle all but the most outrageously air-resistant bugs with ease. If you fish exclusively with small, streamlined bugs, you can cast comfortably with a 5- or 6-weight outfit. If you're a big-bug angler, and if you do a lot of fishing near heavy weeds, a 9- or 10-weight rig will allow you to cast easily, and the powerful rod will turn the heads of big bass that want to tangle you in the thick stuff.

A forward-tapered (weight-forward) line enables you to throw a bug with a minimum of false casting. It sacrifices a bit of distance and some delicacy of presentation (neither of which is usually important in bass bugging), but it loads the rod quickly. The "bass-bug" taper puts even more weight up at the front of the line than the standard weight-forward taper, and makes fast, accurate casting that much easier. You can convert a standard weight-forward or double-tapered line to a bass-bug taper by cutting off the first eight or ten feet.

It should be a floating line, of course. Not only does a floating line keep the bug afloat, but it also enables you to manipulate the bug and lift the line off the water to begin your next cast more easily than you could with a sinking line. Some floating lines float better than others. Several new designs are billed as unsinkable. Any line that refuses to sink is ideal for bass bugging.

After a few hours of casting, even "unsinkable" lines might begin to sink. This happens when the microscopic aquatic growth and other crud that scums the surface of nutrient-rich bass water accumulates on the line. Carry a rag or a square of felt impregnated with line cleaner with you, and whenever your line begins to sink, take a few minutes to dry and clean it.

Lines come in colors ranging from neon green, yellow, orange, and red to neutral shades of gray and brown. There is no evidence that bright-colored floating lines—which appear as dark silhouettes from underwater regardless of their actual color—spook bass (although the flash of a line in the sun over a bass's head *will* spook him). Choose a line that's highly visible to you. On dark days, in twilight, and in shadows, a bright-colored line enables you to locate your bug quickly.

THE LEADER

Bass are not normally leader-shy. The main job of the bass-bug leader is to continue the line's taper, giving you something thin enough at its end to poke through the eye of a hook and tie into a solid knot. A smoothly tapered line-and-leader combination won't collapse on itself or otherwise mess up your casting. For most purposes, a tapered leader between eight and ten feet long, including tippet, that tests at eight to twelve pounds will handle all the bugs you might want to cast and all the bass you might hook. To turn over very large bugs, or to horse bass out of thick weeds, use a leader that tests at fifteen or even twenty pounds. The extra one or two one-thousands of an inch in diameter won't scare off a bass that wants to eat your bug.

A good bass-bug leader should be on the stiff side, with a hard finish. The butt end should be about the same diameter as the end of your fly line for a smooth continuing taper. Leaders come in a variety of more or less transparent colors, but there is no evidence that bass care.

Start with a knotless tapered leader six feet long that tests at twelve pounds and tie two feet of eight- or ten-pound tippet to the end. This is sturdy enough to turn over all but the bulkiest bugs. After changing bugs a few times and throwing a wind knot or two into the tippet, just cut it off and replace it. This way, you should be able to get through a whole season without having to replace the leader itself.

Knotted leaders will pick up weeds and gunk at the knots, a problem that knotless tapered leaders help you avoid.

THE ROD

Today's graphite fly rods come in a bewildering variety of sizes, flexes, designs, and prices. Selecting the "right" one can feel like a major project. The conventional wisdom on the subject generally advocates testing rods until you find the one that matches your casting style and stroke. That is sound advice up to a point, except that for many anglers, smooth, easy bass-bug casting requires some adjustments in style and stroke. Good bugging rods are heavy, long, and relatively "soft."

- **Weight.** The "weight" of a fly rod refers to the line it is designed to cast, not how it tips the scales. An 8-weight rod, for example, is made for an 8-weight line, which is a good all-around choice for bass-bug fishing. Some fishermen find that "overloading" their rod—matching a 9-weight line to an 8-weight rod—makes casting heavy, air-resistant bugs easier.

- **Length.** Standard fly rods range in length from seven to ten feet. Short rods handicap the bass-bug fisherman. A nine- or even ten-foot rod gives you the leverage you need to fight big bass. The long rod also makes it easy to keep your backcast off the water when you're sitting in a canoe, wading up to your waist, or drifting in a float tube, and it enables you to lift your line smoothly off the water to begin your next cast.

- **Flex.** The way a fly rod bends affects how well you can cast with it. For trout fishing with tiny, virtually weightless flies, the most suitable rod flex is largely a matter of your own natural casting stroke, but casting big air-resistant bass bugs demands a slower stroke. A rod that flexes evenly from the tip all the way down to the butt is "slow" or "soft." A slow rod handles bugs nicely if your casting stroke is slow and smooth and if you don't need to cast long distances. On the other extreme, a "fast" or "stiff" rod does most of its bending out toward the tip. A fast rod is powerful, but it's less forgiving of the caster whose timing is imperfect, and its quickness is out of tempo with the slow bug-casting stroke. The "medium-action" rod flexes from the middle through the tip and is the best choice for most bass-bug fishermen. It's strong enough to get the bug and line out there with a minimum of false casting, it suits the slowed-down timing you need to control a bulky bass bug, and it has enough guts to bully a strong bass that is determined to bore into the weeds.

Some rods "track" better than others and are inherently more accurate. This quality is not always reflected in the rod's price. Before you buy a rod, try it out. If it consistently throws curves in your line and lands your fly to one side or the other of where you aim, it doesn't matter whether the flaw lies in the rod or in your casting stroke. Discard that rod and try another.

Expensive rods cost more mostly because they come with prettier wrappings, fancier reel seats, and top-quality hardware. Many low-end rods are made from the same blanks—and therefore cast exactly the same—as the pricier ones produced by the same manufacturer.

If you're a traditionalist, you might be willing to tolerate the shortcomings of a split-bamboo rod for the other pleasures it gives you. But bamboo—and, to a somewhat lesser degree, fiberglass—make inferior bass-bugging rods. Graphite rods are light and strong and worth the investment. A modern high-modulus graphite rod enables you to cast heavy lines and bulky bugs accurately and long distances with minimal effort. The bamboo or fiberglass rod you'd need to handle a bug on an 8-weight line feels like a broomstick next to a comparable graphite rod. Lightness and backbone are important considerations for the comfort of the bass-bug fisherman, who might make several hundred casts in an afternoon.

As with sharp axes and other quality hand tools, a well-balanced casting outfit will do the work for you if you let it.

THE REEL

Expensive reels offer definite advantages for some kinds of fishing. Whenever you expect to encounter hard-running fish such as salmon, big trout, and almost all saltwater species, a reel with a smooth, reliable disc drag that holds a couple of hundred yards of backing can make the difference between catching and losing hooked fish.

For bass bugging, however, the reel serves primarily as a line-storing device. Bass do not run hard, fast, or for long distances. I have never hooked a bass that peeled the entire length of my line off the reel and took me into my backing. Bass will bore for cover when they're hooked. They're strong and dogged fighters, but they're sloggers and jumpers, not high-speed long-distance runners. The rod, not the reel, is your bass-fighting tool.

If you want to save money on your bass-bugging outfit, economize with an inexpensive reel. All you need is something big enough to store the line.

SUNGLASSES

You should *not*, on the other hand, try to economize on sunglasses. High-quality glasses are at least as important to your fishing pleasure as your rod. Good glasses protect your eyes from dangerous UV rays, cut surface glare, deflect stray hooks, keep wind and sand from blowing into your eyes, prevent headaches, and enable you to spot fish and study the bottom through the water's surface. Poor glasses can be worse than not wearing glasses at all.

The best sunglasses are made from ophthalmic glass, which is distortion-free and scratch-resistant. Some of today's plastic lenses are almost as good. Aside from the fact that you can pay extra for style and brand name, it's pretty much true that with sunglasses, you get what you pay for.

Here are the qualities to look for in sunglasses:

- **100 percent UV protection.** The sun's UV rays can permanently damage your eyes. Quality sunglasses are rated for UV protection. Don't skimp here.

- **Zero distortion.** Distortion will cause eyestrain and headaches. You can test a pair of glasses for distortion simply by holding them away from your face and rotating them. If what you see through them appears to move or change shape, don't buy them. Cheap sunglasses are cheap because, among other things, they're poorly made and are not distortion-free.

- **Polarized lenses** cut the sun's reflective glare off the water's surface, increasing both your comfort and your ability to see down into the water.

- **Color.** Different-colored lenses do different jobs. Shades of orange (yellow, amber, copper, vermilion, brown) filter out some colors more than others, increasing contrast and making underwater objects such as fish and structure sharp and easy to see. Shades of gray, blue, and green are neutral filters, reducing all colors equally. Amber is best for all-around fishing use. For low-light conditions, go with yellow. In intense sunlight, brown is best.

- **Photochromic lenses** adjust to the available light, becoming lighter in low-light conditions and darker in bright sun, providing optimum vision all the time.

- **Comfort.** Glass lenses are heavier than plastic, but if they fit properly, you won't notice their weight. Sunglasses should have adjustable frames that fit your nose and ears comfortably and do not slip.

- **Side shields** are plastic or leather attachments that shade your eyes around the edges of the lenses and provide additional protection and comfort.

- **Lanyards.** Affix a "croakie" or some other kind of lanyard to the ends of the stems, so that if your glasses slip off your nose, you won't step on them or lose them in the water.

CLOTHING

Your mother has already taught you to dress warmly when it's cold outside and to wear rain gear when it's wet. But if she neglected to educate you about sun protection, here are some sobering facts to ponder:

- More than one million Americans are stricken with some form of skin cancer every year, and more than nine thousand die from it.

- Skin cancer is the most common type of malignancy. It's increasing among Americans at a rate of 3 percent annually.

- Virtually all skin cancers are caused by UV radiation from the sun and are entirely preventable.

- A T-shirt or any loosely woven fabric has an SPF (sun protection factor) of only 5. When it's wet, its SPF is reduced to 2, which means you are going virtually bareback.

- Clouds and haze do not filter out all UV rays. You can get a serious dose of UV radiation even on a rainy day.

- The dangers of UV radiation are increasing steadily as the earth's ozone layer, which works as a filter, continues to deteriorate.

- The earth's atmosphere filters out more UV radiation when the sun's rays are sharply angled, such as in early morning, late afternoon, and in the winter. UV rays also reflect off water. Midsummer, midday fishing on a sunny day is therefore the most dangerous time.

Hold your shirt up to the light. If you can see light through it, the fabric will not keep UV rays off your skin. Loomed cotton or—even better—layers of clothing will protect you. Some fabrics are specifically designed for sun protection. Look for fabrics with an SPF of 30. To be safe, apply sunscreen before you get dressed.

Your long-billed baseball cap shades your eyes but does not shield your face, nose, ears, or neck from the sun. Wear a hat with a solid (not mesh) four-inch brim all around.

OTHER IMPORTANT STUFF

When you want to prowl or wade along the shoreline of a bass pond or creek, you can carry everything you need in your shirt pockets or a fanny pack. In a rowboat or canoe, stow it all in a waterproof canvas bag. In addition to rod and reel, these are the necessities:

- One sturdy ventilated plastic fly box with large compartments for your bugs. Even if you own hundreds of bass bugs, there's never a reason to carry more than a dozen or so with you. Cramming too many bugs into a box crushes them. Drill a few holes in the box, so that when you put back a wet bug, the moisture can evaporate. Otherwise you'll end up with a boxful of rusty hooks.

- A spool of eight- to twelve-pound tippet material.

- A pair of needle-nose pliers for debarbing hooks and releasing deeply hooked fish unharmed.

- Scissors for cutting leaders and reshaping deerhair bugs.

- A tube of SPF-30 broad-spectrum sunscreen. Lather it onto all exposed skin first thing, and reapply it every couple of hours.

- Flashlights. If you expect to be out after dark—which might be anytime you set forth in the afternoon—carry two lights: a small, narrow-focus one for knot tying, and a stronger one for lighting your way off the water and packing away your gear.

  Several useful knot-tying lights are available that are designed to leave both hands free. There are lights you can clench in your teeth, lights that attach to the bill of your cap, lights that clip onto the front of your shirt, and even lights that clinch around your thumb. Pick one that works for you, and be sure not to shine it on the water. Sudden flashes of light at night can spook bass.

  For unloading your gear and walking through the woods at night, a headlamp always aims in the right direction and keeps both hands free for more important functions like lugging and loading gear and pushing aside brush.

- Insect repellent.

- A plastic bottle for drinking water.

THE COMPLEAT BUG BOX

If you want to travel extra-light, such as when you're wading or prowling a shoreline on foot, leave the bug box home and stick half a dozen flat-faced Tap's Bugs into your hat—two big ones (size 2/0), two medium ones (size 2), and two small ones (size 6). If you feel you want a slimmer bug, or a rounded-off face that makes less of a fuss on the water, simply trim and reshape it with scissors.

My devotion to my father's invention is not a matter of blind filial loyalty. Many other bass-bug addicts feel the same way I do about Tap's Bug. Jack Ellis, for example, says: "This bug is rarely tied today because it just doesn't satisfy our aesthetic inclinations, but I can assure you that it will take as many bass as the fanciest creation from the vise of the most famous fly tier. As we have seen, pattern rarely matters in bass bugging. It's the action the angler imparts to the bug that counts, and an assortment of these basic bugs in several colors and sizes is all the practical angler needs. In fact, a simple Tap's Bug, tied with natural deer hair on a size 1/0 hook, will do the job anywhere, anytime."

By all means, you should use the bugs you have faith in. Any assortment that includes a few different sizes, shapes, and movable parts will take bass under virtually all conditions.

In addition to a few Tap's Bugs, and depending on the water I'm fishing, these are the bugs I generally carry in my box:

The compleat bass-bug box.

- **Art Scheck's In-Betweener.** This all-synthetic foam bug is halfway between a slider and a popper. In size 6, it's big enough to entice any bass and small enough to fit into the mouths of decent-sized bluegills and crappies. It's what I tie on when I expect to catch panfish but want to get the attention of any bass that might see it. A good choice for leisurely midday bugging.

- **Roy Yates's Deacon.** This Muddler look-alike is the easiest to cast of all the bass-sized bugs I use. I like it for its subtlety in glass-flat shallow water. It lands softly, rides low, and burbles gently when twitched—just enough to attract a nearby bass, but not so much as to frighten even the most skittish fish.

- **Gartside's Gurgler.** This foam invention of master tier Jack Gartside is a proven bass taker. It casts easily, kicks up a commotion, and floats forever. It's so quick and easy to tie that I don't mourn its loss when a toothy pickerel or pike shreds it, so it's my choice for water where I expect an encounter with one of those toothy gamefish.

- **Dahlberg's Diver.** This deerhair bug is designed to dive under the surface when it's retrieved, then pop back up when at rest. It's a good option over deep water or whenever the bass seem particularly lethargic.

- **Deerhair mouse.** I don't actually expect to need to match the mouse hatch, but sometimes it's fun to bounce a fake mouse off the bank.

- **Hair Frog.** Bass don't feed selectively on frogs, either, but they rarely spurn one that ventures too close. Anyway, I doubt that when a bass spots a Hair Frog, he thinks, "Aha! A frog!" The rubber arms and splayed hackle legs on the Hair Frog make it a good choice for pockets in a bed of lily pads or among the branches of waterlogged trees, where you don't have much room for a retrieve and want the tiniest twitch to set the bug to vibrating and wiggling—which is what triggers that bass's predatory reaction.

- **Hard-bodied popper.** For wind-riffled or deep water, large flat-faced poppers make the most ruckus and attract fish that might not notice a less noisy hair bug. Big poppers are normally the only hard-bodied bugs I carry with me.

Tactics, Techniques, and Tricks

> "They [bass bugs] should not be retrieved rapidly. Rather, after they have been dropped on the water one should let them lie there a moment before moving them at all. Then they should be made to quiver a bit by twitching the rod tip after which the retrieve may be started."
> Ray Bergman, *Just Fishing* (1932)

> "The advantage of a lightly dropped bug is that it causes less disturbance than other lures and can be allowed to rest motionless on the water long enough to capture the interest of the fish."
> Joe Brooks, *Bass Bug Fishing* (1947)

> "The fast retrieve with its greater surface commotion frequently stirs up fish that might lose interest in a motionless bug."
> H. G. Tapply, *The Sportsman's Notebook* (1964)

I converted Mr. Bass from a lip-rippin' buzzbait-and-rubber-worm tournament champion to a fly-rod bass-bug fanatic in a couple of early-morning hours about fifteen years ago.

Mr. Bass had earned his coveted title by catching more and bigger bass than anyone else in tournaments all over New England. He represented that new generation of high-tech bassers (a word that can be usefully mispronounced) who had driven me away from my favorite bass waters.

I didn't know him well at the time, but I found him to be an amiable guy and modest about his accomplishments. Those who had lost championships to him told me he was an extremely fierce competitor, a monofilament magician, and the master of a bewildering array of bass hardware. This was to be our first fishing trip together. I figured I'd learn something.

He had one of those bass boats that I'd come to curse. It was powered from behind by a fifty-horse Mercury and from the front by a foot-operated electric motor. An electronic device sketched the contours of the bottom and displayed shapes that represented actual fish. The boat bristled with spinning and bait-casting rods, each rigged with a different sort of lure. He wanted to be ready for any situation, Mr. Bass told me. He brought two tackle boxes, each the size of a footlocker.

When I showed up lugging one 8-weight graphite fly rod in my left hand and one plastic box of deerhair bugs in my right, his eyebrows arched and his mouth twitched. He was too polite to say it, but I knew what he was thinking: "Oh, Lord. Another one of those effete fly-rod snobs who will claim to get more pleasure from casting artistically and admiring the sunrise than from catching fish."

I think Mr. Bass hoped to convert me. I certainly had no intention of converting him.

The July sky was just turning from black to purple and the stars had begun to wink out when we launched his boat. The water lay as flat and dark as a mug of camp coffee, fuzzed by the faint twilight mist that rose from its surface. Mr. Bass perched on the high front seat. He steered the boat with the foot-operated electric and probed the brushy shoreline with a spin-cast rubber worm. I cast a deerhair bug from the stern, taking his leavings.

We'd been casting for about fifteen minutes when the water underneath my bug suddenly erupted. Moments earlier, Mr. Bass had snaked his worm though the same place without a strike. I lip-landed the largemouth. He weighed a shade under three pounds. "Nice fish," muttered Mr. Bass. He put down his spinning rod and picked up a bait-casting rig armed with something lethal-looking that he called a "stickbait."

Mr. Bass eased the electric into super-slow as we approached a deliciously bassy deadfall. Almost instantly he hooked a bass on his stickbait. After he had maneuvered his fish into deeper water, I cast my bug against the same half-submerged tree. I twitched it once, making it burble softly, let it sit, then twitched it again.

Mr. Bass landed his largemouth, weighed him, and slipped him back into the water. "Three and a half," he said matter-of-factly.

At which exact instant my bug disappeared in a washtub-sized swirl. A moment later, the bass vaulted into the air. "Mm," murmured Mr. Bass. "Pretty nice one."

A shade over four pounds, as it turned out.

We fished out that length of shoreline, and while I steered the big motor to the next hot spot, Mr. Bass rummaged among his bundle of rods. When I cut the motor to drift into a lily-padded cove, he said, "Uh, can I try one of those things?"

He had a fly rod in his hand. I tossed him my box of bugs.

At the next waterlogged tree, he landed a five-pounder on his fly rod, and I caught a four-and-a-half-pounder from the same hole.

We were home by eight-thirty that morning. We had caught twenty pounds of largemouth bass in a little over two hours. Sixteen and a half of those pounds came to deerhair bass bugs fished on the surface with a fly rod.

Mr. Bass was (and still is) Andy Gill, with whom I cemented an angling partnership that July morning fifteen-odd years ago. I don't really take credit (if that's the word) for the fact that he gave up competitive fishing, sold his bass boat, stuffed his trophies in a closet, and began trekking all over North America with me, armed only with fly rods. Andy, like me, had fished obsessively all his life for whatever species he encountered and with any tool that would catch them. He'd watched bobbers and cast plugs and spinning lures and flies. He already was a masterful dry-fly trout angler when I met him. So it was probably inevitable that sooner or later he'd rediscover the old-fashioned fun of bass-bug fishing and, when he did, that he'd prefer it to tournaments and electronics and treble hooks. But I still like to claim that I converted him, and he's good-natured enough not to contradict me.

Bass-bug fishing is decidedly low-tech, easygoing, and stripped-down. Toss almost anything that floats over almost any shallow water, make it move a little, and sooner or later a bass will try to eat it.

Catching bass on bugs is pretty simple. Doing it consistently is harder.

GETTING THERE

Bass boats are designed for the job, and while their gadgets and mechanics and electronics strike me as incompatible with fly-rod bug fishing, there is no denying their efficiency. In a bass boat you can scoot from the north end of a good-sized lake to that sheltered shoreline on the south end without wasting a lot of fishing time, and then, with its shallow draft and weedless electric motor, you can prowl coves and creep along the edges of weed beds, steering with your foot to leave both hands free for casting.

The main practical disadvantage of bass boats (aside from their cost) is their inflexibility. You simply cannot fish any river, pond, or lake that doesn't have a launch area where you can back your trailer into the water.

Wooden rowboats are relatively impractical bass-stalking craft. They're heavy, awkward, uncomfortable, and slow-moving even with a motor mounted on the transom. They tend to leak, their oarlocks usually groan, and unless you keep yours moored on your favorite pond or lake, you need a trailer to get it into the water, making all those lightly fished bass hot spots without launching facilities inaccessible.

However, my first memories of bass-bug fishing are of taking turns at the oars with my father, and in my imagination, rowboats and bass bugs still belong together. They are both old-timey and low-tech. Casting bugs to a shoreline from a rowboat seems to tap into something utterly comfortable and evocative. "In the evenings," writes Nick Lyons, "even before I could use the long rod with any semblance of skill, we would row quietly down the lake, parallel to the shoreline, and cast in against the rocks and grasses and deadfalls for largemouth bass." I have those same nostalgic feelings about rowboats.

Canoes are more portable and, especially with a small outboard mounted on the transom of a square-ender, swifter than rowboats. With its shallow draft, you can go about anywhere in a canoe. A thirteen-foot aluminum canoe weighs about forty-five pounds, light enough for a pair of intrepid bass fishermen, taking turns, to carry for miles on their shoulders into remote, secret ponds. Canoes are ideal watercraft for two anglers who enjoy taking turns on a small body of water. They are less stable than rowboats, however, and trying to paddle and hold a position and cast a fly rod all at the same time is more than one man can handle.

For the stealthiest possible approach, you can't beat a float tube. From a tube, you can work your way along a shoreline in virtual silence, and your low profile enables you to paddle close to likely cover without the risk of spooking fish. You can launch a tube anywhere you can walk to—they are lightweight and easy to carry. Depending on the water temperature, you don't even need to wear waders. A bathing suit keeps you cool on a summer bass pond, although if you're leery of leeches or at all spooky about mysterious underwater creatures, you'll be more comfortable in a pair of lightweight waders or quick-drying trousers.

Because you travel backward in a tube, the best strategy for right-handed casters is to move counterclockwise (clockwise, of course, for a left-handed caster) around a pond. You move and steer by kicking your finned feet. Maneuvering a float tube with fins is absolutely instinctive (although climbing into and out of one without embarrassing yourself takes practice). No matter how hard you kick, you will barely chug along, so it's not worth trying to go fast or cover a lot of water. In a tube, you fish slow and thorough—which is the way a bass bug should be fished anyway.

Tubes are ideal for small ponds, sluggish rivers, and other intimate bodies of water whose shorelines feature more or less continuous bass cover. But even the one-man, half-tube/half-boat craft that come equipped with oars are slow and inefficient wherever you might want to cover a lot of water or move significant distances between hot spots.

Wading and bank-stalking bass is more trouble than it's worth on the steep, weedy, brush-clogged, mud-bottomed shorelines that characterize much bass water. But wherever the bottom is firm and gravelly and gently sloping, try fishing unencumbered by any kind of boat. Tiptoe up to the bank and stop well back from the edge. Peer hard into the water before stepping in, to be sure you don't overlook a bass you might catch. Then begin to make short casts in a fanlike pattern, starting parallel to the bank and moving outward with each successive cast. After you cover that water thoroughly, begin to stalk your way along the shoreline. Pick your targets—alleys and potholes in the weeds, underwater rocks, stickups and stubs, drop-offs and depressions in the bottom, edges of all kinds.

You can cover all the bassy water on foot, and with polarized glasses you can study it better than you can from a boat. Play the heron. If you do a lot of standing still and looking, you'll hardly ever spook a fish. It's like still-hunting deer or squirrels. You'll enjoy feeling intimate with the water, really getting to know it. It might take you a few hours to cover a hundred yards of shoreline, but you might see lots of bass. Experience will teach you what to look for—shapes, swirls, wakes, shadows, sometimes just a subtle twitch of the reeds or a humping movement under a lily pad. If you go slow and watch where you step, you can usually creep up close to them. And you're so low to the water that they can't see you.

Wading the shallows or even casting from shore gives bass a different—and more natural—look at the bug. As Charles Waterman writes, "So much bass fishing is done with a lure thrown near cover and pulled away from it that we sometimes forget the exact opposite can be effective. Some of my best fishing for largemouths involved casting from near the bank out across a bed of weeds and bringing a bug, streamer, or nymph back toward the cover. Almost anything a bass wants to eat is likely to seek refuge in cover rather than flee from it, and 'pinning bait against the weeds' is an old bass stratagem."

The best part of wade fishing is that you can fish places that no boat can get into—tiny potholes and creeks and backwaters and ponds, places you have to bushwhack into that are too far from the road even for portaging a tube or little canoe comfortably.

STEALTH

Regardless of whether you travel by boat, canoe, tube, or foot, if bass know you're there, it's unlikely you'll catch any of them. They are as quick to flee any sudden or unnatural motion, sound, or flash of light as bonefish and trout are, especially in shallow water where they feel most vulnerable—and where bass-bug fishermen hunt them.

Trout, which always face upstream in moving water, can usually be approached very closely from behind. But you never know which way a stillwater bass might be looking. A few simple precautions will increase your chances of casting to where bass are lurking, not the place from which they've recently fled:

- **Wear drab-colored shirts and hats,** especially when stalking bass from shore. I prefer shades of gray, green, and brown.

- **Keep a low profile.** A float tube automatically provides a low profile. From a boat you'll hit your targets more regularly if you approach close, remain sitting, and make short casts rather than trying long-distance casts while standing up or perched high on a swivel seat. When wading or prowling the shoreline, move slowly, hunch down, stay in the shadows, and keep bushes or the bank behind you to break up your outline.

- **Avoid noise.** Sound travels a long distance in still water, and bass come with finely tuned sound-detecting equipment. Just as they will swim over from far away to investigate something that drops softly onto the water and vibrates quietly (such as a moth . . . or a deerhair bug), so will they flee from the source of any noise that translates as danger.

  You can't be absolutely quiet in any boat. Bass cannot hear voices, so you can hoot and holler all you want. But bass will hear the scrape of a foot on the bottom, the bump of a paddle against a gunwale, the clank of an oarlock, even the buzz of an electric motor. I'm not sure how much particular sounds actually bother bass, and I suspect they tolerate some more than others. But any unnatural sound will surely make them nervous, and I'm quite sure that the best sound of all is silence.

- **Avoid flash and shadow.** When the sun is at a low angle— toward sunrise or sunset—your long shadow moving across the water will spook fish. Even when your profile and shadow are beyond a bass's cone of vision, there's your fly rod waving high over the water, and if the sun's coming from the right—or, to be more precise, the wrong—angle, fish will be startled by the reflected light. Be aware of the sun and, if necessary, either move to a better position or drop your rod and cast sidearm. Similarly, waving your line over the water can create a moving shadow or flash that will spook shallow-water fish. Make your false casts to the side of your intended target.

- **Beware of scents.** Although bass hunt topwater lures such as bugs primarily by sight and sound, any strong unnatural scent will deter them from trying to eat them. Particularly noxious to bass are gasoline, insect repellent, sunscreen, and human perspiration. Take the simple precaution of rinsing your hands in the water before handling and tying on your bug.

CASTING

Fishermen who are used to casting tiny trout flies on lightweight rods usually find bass-bug casting awkward and laborious, at least at first. Even the smallest, lightest, and most streamlined bugs are considerably heavier and more air-resistant than trout flies. Casting them efficiently and accurately requires the right equipment and good timing.

Nobody can cast a bass bug efficiently if his fly line is too light to overcome the bulk of the bug, or if his rod doesn't match his line. In fact, no outfit is too heavy to handle a bass bug, but it can certainly be too light. The rig you need to move a big, bulky bug through the air will also cast a tiny bug easily.

Unless you want to carry several outfits with you, the rule of thumb is: Choose an outfit that will handle the biggest, least-aerodynamic bug you might want to tie on. If you intend to cast only bluegill-sized bugs, a 5- or 6-weight outfit will do the job and save your shoulder from heavy labor. An 8-weight line will handle most bass-sized bugs and is a good all-around choice. But if you sometimes enjoy targeting trophy-sized largemouths with sparrow-sized bugs, make a 9- or 10-weight outfit your bass-bugging weapon.

A heavy line with a bulky bug tied to the tippet, even on a powerful rod, moves through the air more slowly than a thin trout-weight line. The tip-action rod and the quick, wristy casting stroke that work well for false casting and air-drying a trout-sized dry fly spell disaster for bass bugging. A medium-action rod and a slow, smooth casting stroke work together to give the heavy bugging line time to straighten out on your back- and forward casts. Resist the impulse to compensate by trying to overpower the weight of the line and the bug or by speeding up your stroke. The best way to find the right timing is to watch your backcast over your shoulder. Don't begin your forward stroke until you see that the line has straightened out behind you. Soon you'll learn to feel the line loading the rod, and you won't need to look.

With the right outfit and the proper timing, you'll have no trouble casting a bass bug as far as you'll ever need to. Smooth, easy casting is just a matter of rhythm and letting the rod and line do their job. If you find yourself straining to reach bassy targets with your bug, simply move closer. There's rarely any reason to cast more than fifty feet.

Recognizing likely bass targets and hitting them consistently with a well-cast bug, more than any other factor—including the bug you choose to fish with—are what separate successful bass-bug fishermen from everyone else. Accuracy is more important than delicacy in bass-bug casting, although there are times when both are desirable. Even big, bulky deerhair bugs hit the water with a natural-sounding, fish-attracting splat. Unless you drop it directly atop a basking bass, that splat is more likely to attract a nearby fish than spook him.

Fly casting is inherently more accurate than other methods of delivering a lure. A reasonably competent fly caster can hit the bull's-eye more consistently than all but the elite bait or spin casters, which is one big advantage we have over those high-tech folks. False casting allows us to fine-tune our distance before we drop our bug onto the water, and we can pull back a cast at the last instant if we realize it's destined to be off target. But don't false cast excessively. The flash and shadow of a line in the air can spook a bass.

Bass usually hold tight to bankside logs, rocks, and weed beds and under overhanging limbs, bushes, and docks. They do not like to move far from their cover to eat. If you want to entice them to eat your bug, you've got to put it close to them, so cast aggressively. If you don't occasionally overshoot your target, you're probably being too cautious.

Work on casting hard, tight loops that enable you to drive your bug through light foliage. By dropping your rod to a horizontal position, you can make a forceful sidearm cast that will cause a deerhair bug to bounce off the water's surface and skip under low overhanging cover.

Another advantage we fly casters enjoy over our spinning and bait-casting counterparts is the ability to make another cast as soon as we've fished the productive water. There's rarely any need to retrieve a bug all the way to the boat. Work your bug through the good-looking water, usually no more than halfway back to you, then pick up your line and begin your next cast.

If you don't do it right, bass bugs, especially those with wide, flat faces, will dig into the water's surface when you try to lift them off, ruining your next cast and making an explosive noise that will send every bass in the pond scurrying for cover.

To start your next cast, don't try to get the bug airborne until most of your line is off the water. First be sure that your rod is pointing at the bug and your line is straight. Then raise your rod smoothly, while simultaneously pulling back on the line with your line hand. This will lift your line off the water before the bug and start it moving into a smooth, strong backcast.

PUTTING THE BUG TO WORK

Old-time bug fishermen were almost unanimous in their insistence that you couldn't retrieve a bug slowly enough. The common rule of thumb in those politically incorrect days was: After your bug hits the water, lay your rod across your lap, light a cigarette, and smoke the entire thing before giving the bug its first twitch. Nonsmokers ate sandwiches.

Harold F. Blaisdell in *Tricks That Take Fish* tried to imagine how bass think: "You can bet your bottom dollar that he saw your bug drop to the water and is watching it now as it lies motionless. Why doesn't he take it? Bass just aren't built that way. As long as it lies still he knows he can nail it; maybe he finds little sporting appeal in a sure thing. Move it? Not yet—let him work up to a state of readiness. He wants that bug to move, never fear. The longer he has to wait, the more likely he'll be to murder it at the first suggestion of attempted escape."

In *Black Bass*, John Alden Knight made the same argument: "When I'm fishing a bug in placid water, I rarely begin the retrieve until the ring that is caused by the bug striking the surface is about ten feet in diameter. If you hold your pace down to about that rate, you will find that you get more bass than you will if you hurry."

And Joe Brooks in *Bass Bug Fishing* wrote: "The slower the retrieve, the better. When you drop your bug on the water, stifle the desire to pop it back as quickly as possible and get off another cast. When it hits, let it stay where it is from one-half to almost a minute. Then give it a slight twitch with your rod tip, or even pop it. Let it stay motionless again for half a minute. Another twitch or pop. Play it back in a series of pops. Pick it up and cast again."

There is no question that this patient waiting game often works. It's a lot easier to execute when your bug has landed beside a shady downfall or in a pothole surrounded by lily pads where you just *know* a big bass is lurking. When you're working your way down a shoreline, however, and a particularly bassy cove lies just around the next point, spending several minutes to fish out each cast requires superhuman willpower—while in the back of your mind, you suspect you might be wasting precious fishing time that could be better invested in certified hot spots.

Rarely do tournament bass fishermen favor the super-slow retrieve. In fact, they generally just chuck it out and chug it back. They vary the speed and rhythm of their retrieve depending on the lure and,

I'm sure, a vast array of other variables known only to them. But they do like to keep the thing moving.

If waiting a minute before giving their lure its first twitch would catch more bass, you can be sure that when prize money is on the line, the professional bass catchers would do it that way.

We tend to impute human characteristics to the fish we hunt. We believe they have "moods," that they can be "angered" into striking, that they are susceptible to "teasing" or "tormenting," or that they can be "stubborn" or "cautious." Maybe, maybe not. The fact is, most of the time bass simply do what their instincts drive them to do to survive: They spawn when the urge is upon them, they seek shelter and comfortable water, they flee from danger . . . and they eat.

Natural bass foods don't all behave the same way, and there's no reason to think that the fish prefer one behavior over another. A grasshopper usually begins to kick desperately the instant it hits the water. A mouse begins swimming as soon as it splashes down. A moth flaps its wings for a moment before lying still. A frog swims, pauses to look around, then swims some more. An injured or disoriented baitfish churns around the surface. Nearby bass will devour any one of these bits of nourishment with equal enthusiasm.

The message for the bass-bug fisherman is: By all means, vary the speed and cadence of your retrieve, but don't waste a lot of time fishing over water that might be barren. I catch a lot of bass—especially, for some reason, smallmouths—by beginning my retrieve as soon as my bug hits the water and keeping it coming steadily back in a series of forceful twitches and jerks, which Dave Whitlock calls the "panic strip." It works especially well over deep-water bass cover such as reefs, sunken weed beds, and drowned timber, where you need to grab and hold the attention of fish that will have to swim up from the bottom to strike. I have also found the panic strip effective when casting to bass on their spawning beds.

My father, as usual, offered sensible advice in *The Sportsman's Notebook:* "If you insist on a rule to govern this situation, try the slow retrieve in pockets where you feel certain a good bass should be hiding, the fast retrieve when you are fishing blind in open water."

And Harold Blaisdell, writing in *The Philosophical Fisherman* fifteen years after advocating the motionless tease, had apparently given the entire business a second thought. Harold and Dad did a lot of fishing together, and sometimes I was allowed to tag along. I heard them argue and debate all manner of arcane subjects, not all of which concerned fishing. But I do know they learned a lot from each other—including how to catch bass on bugs. "It is true," Blaisdell wrote in his second book, "that bass will hit a motionless bug, but it probably would be nearer the truth to say that they do so in spite of its lack of motion, rather than because of it. . . . Actually, when bass are in the mood to come to popping bugs, it is as impossible to hit on a presentation to which they won't respond as it is to arrive at one which is demonstrably superior."

One of the advantages of deerhair bass bugs is the variety of noises and movements you can impart to them, all the way from subtle vibrations to loud, attention-grabbing pops. Leave it motionless, vibrate it, and let it lie. Try a twitch-pause-twitch retrieve, or vary it by alternating a hard strip with a pause. Mix and match. Try them all. Some days one method seems to work better than others, but I suspect that most of the time, it makes less difference than many experts claim. A hungry bass will eat. If he's not hungry, it may take more than a tantalizing bass bug to change his mind. Yes, you might be able to anger or otherwise persuade him, and if you're convinced he's there and he's a big one, it's worth trying—in which case, the fast, steady retrieve is just as likely to induce him to strike as that agonizingly slow waiting game.

Regardless of the kind of movement you give your bug or the speed of your retrieve, **always keep your rod tip pointing directly at the bug. Manipulate the bug by tugging on the line—not by twitching or jerking the rod itself.** Maintaining a straight line down the rod, line, and leader all the way to your bug keeps you in control. A one-inch tug on the line moves the bug one inch. Tug hard and the bug pops. Tug gently and it twitches and vibrates.

Moving the bug by lifting your rod or yanking it sideways creates slack in your line that leaves you out of control and could cost you a hookup. By keeping your rod tip low and the line straight, you are ready for a strike at all times.

Be sure the bottom of the boat between your feet is clear of stray tackle, protruding nuts and bolts, and other odds and ends that will catch your stripped-in line and short-circuit your casts—always at the worst possible time. Float tubes generally come equipped with an apron that spreads across your lap to hold your line. When you're casting from the shore or wading in weedy or brushy water, a stripping basket will prevent foul-ups and give you control of your loose line.

FISHING THE WATER

If you're fishing from a boat or a float tube and you've come upon a bed of lily pads, a big deadfall, or a rocky shoal, the rule of thumb is "outside in." Make short casts to the water closest to you first, then gradually move closer or lengthen your casts. For example, cast first to the outermost tip of a fallen tree, then with successive casts work your way in toward its trunk. This way, the bass you hook on the outside won't spook those that are lying in toward the bank. Fish the near edges of a weed bed or shoal or other large bass-holding area before working your bug out over them.

When fishing from shore, of course, do it the opposite way—inside out. Fish the water closest to you—the base of that fallen tree, the near edge of the weed bed—before you make longer casts out over deeper water.

In rivers and streams, bass seek out comfortable cushions of soft water close to the swifter currents that carry food—along the banks, near boulders, inside current seams, in slow-moving pools. Concentrate on casting to these bassy places. You'll often have to cast your bug across fast currents to reach the slower fish-holding water beyond. To keep your bug in the prime water as long as possible, throw a big upstream mend in your line and move the bug just enough to make it appear alive.

Another effective river tactic is to cover the water methodically. Chugging a bass bug across the current, past boulders and other structure, and over long slow pools often brings bass zooming up from the bottom. Begin at the head of a pool or run, make an across-and-down cast, wake the bug back, take two steps downstream, and cast again. When the current creates a big belly in your line, correct it with an upstream mend. A straight line from rod tip to bug enables you to control the movement of the bug across varied currents and to set the hook when a bass hits.

SETTING THE HOOK

I have emphasized the importance of keeping your rod pointed at your bug and your line straight during the retrieve and when picking up your line to make another cast. Dave Whitlock calls it "the straight-line system," and it's equally important when a fish takes your bug. By maintaining direct control of your line, you should hook most of the bass that you entice into striking.

Bass have strong jaws. They can clamp down on a bug or leader so hard that even with tension on the line, it won't move in their mouths. Unlike trout and many other fish, bass rarely hook themselves. To prevent the fish from opening his mouth and spitting out your bug, you must make a hard, positive hook set. This is what tournament fishermen call, inelegantly and, we hope, inaccurately, "ripping their lips."

When your bug disappears in a big swirl, resist the impulse to raise your rod tip as you might for hooking trout on a small fly and light leader. The rod tip is designed to absorb shock, not drive a large hook into the bony mouth of a bass. Instead, keep your rod tip pointing at the fish and give a hard pull straight back on the line. When you feel the fish's resistance, give it another sharp pull. Then haul up and back with the butt of your rod, using your whole arm, not your wrist. This drives home the hook and puts your rod at the proper angle for fighting the fish.

FIGHTING BASS

Bass are strong and stubborn fighters, but if they're solidly hooked, you should land all of them. Your goal, once you've hooked one, should be to get him in fast, unhook him quickly, and return him to the water before he's exhausted, so that he will recover quickly. This means that you should be aggressive. Don't think of it as "playing" your fish. Take charge. *Fight* him. Force him to come to you.

The trick to fighting a large bass—or any strong fish—is to prevent him from doing what he wants to do. Keep turning his head by moving your rod down and sideways in the opposite direction from the one he's chosen. If he wants to burrow deep, lift him. If he heads for a weed bed or other tangle, go "down and dirty," using the whole bend of your rod to stop and turn him.

Hooked bass like to jump. When they do, the risk is that they'll fall on the taut leader, either breaking it or tearing the bug from their mouths. So when a fish jumps, "bow" to him—bend forward, lower your rod, and push it toward him. This creates enough slack in your line and leader to prevent you and your bass from coming disconnected.

When you've got a large bass on, it's always a good idea to reel in your slack line and fight him off the reel. Early in the encounter, when he's still strong, he might insist on making a short run. If he's heading for open water, let him go. Hold your rod at about eleven o'clock and make him pull against the bend of the rod and the drag of your reel. The fly rod is an excellent lever, and pulling against its insistent bend will tire a fish quickly. When you feel him weaken, pump him in by lifting your rod and reeling in as you lower it.

WHY THE BIG ONES GET AWAY

I have failed to land my share of big fish of many species—including bass—although in my experience, bass are not particularly resourceful or powerful fighters for their size. They like to jump, bulldog, and dive for cover, but they do not make long-distance runs. They tire quickly, and the aggressive angler can usually overpower them. We should never lose a well-hooked and aggressively fought bass.

But we do.

Every time I've hooked and failed to land a big bass, it's been the result of my own carelessness. If he got loose by wrapping the leader around a stub or the anchor line or tangling himself in the weeds, it's because I did not assert myself aggressively enough. If the hook pulled free, I did not set it firmly.

Well, most of us don't get enough practice fighting really big fish, and those things happen.

But there are other reasons for losing fish that are inexcusable. Believe me, I know.

- **Bad knots.** There's nothing more disheartening than to have your line abruptly go slack in the middle of fighting a large fish, then to reel in and find your bug gone and a pigtail at the end of your tippet. No well-tied Trilene, improved clinch, or other standard angling knot should pull loose. Only badly tied knots fail. Tie them carefully, lubricate them with spit before pulling them tight, and leave a little stub when you clip the end. Test your knots regularly. Pay equal attention to the knots that join your tippet to the leader and your leader to the line. Don't hesitate to retie dubious knots.

- **Bad hooks.** Check the bend and point of your hook periodically. Keep a file handy for touching up the point and keeping it needle-sharp. If you cast aggressively, as you should, your bug will bounce off a rock, dock, or log now and then, which can dull or bend the point and prevent a solid hookup. If you hook a log, tugging to pull your bug free could open the bend of the hook enough to weaken it and let a bass slip free. Once a hook is bent, it's permanently weakened, so rather than trying to bend it back, discard that bug and tie on a new one.

- **Bad tippet.** Encounters with toothy fish like pickerel and pike, a worn or scored tiptop rod guide, and even general wear and tear can create nicked or frayed spots on your tippet, converting ten-pound test into ten-ounce. "Wind knots" (overhand knots that are usually caused by a messed-up cast, not the wind) severely weaken a tippet. Run your tippet between your fingertips or, even better, between your lips now and then, and if you feel a nick or wind knot, retie it. It takes only a moment, and tippet material is a lot easier to come by than five-pound bass.

CATCH-AND-RELEASE

In most waters, there's no reason not to keep a bass for the table now and then. If you enjoy bass fillets, kill and eat the small ones and return the lunkers to the water so they can pass along their trophy genes to the next bass generation. Small ones are at least as good eating as big ones, and knowing that a few lunkers still live in your pond definitely leaves a pleasant taste in your mouth.

Some Favorite Bugs

Tap's Bug

Roy Yates's Deacon

All bass bugs tied by author. Photographs by Dick Talleur.

Gerbubble Bug

Feathered Minnow

Dahlberg Diver

Frog

Mouse

Devil Bug

Gartside's Gurgler

Art Scheck's In-Betweener

Catch-and-release is mandated in bass tournaments, and it should also be the usual practice of bug fishermen. If you don't know how to fight, land, unhook, and return a bass without injuring or killing him, you don't deserve to catch him.

- **You're the boss.** Fighting a hooked fish aggressively is the first step to assuring him of a continued healthy life. The longer he's out there thrashing around on the end of your line, the greater the chance that you'll return him to the water exhausted, susceptible to disease, and easy pickings for a predator. Especially when water temperatures hover around the high end of a bass's comfort zone, a fish "played" to exhaustion might not recover. Nothing saddens the angler—or at least this one—more than watching a big fish he's just released turn belly-up and sink slowly out of sight. Fighting a fish to death shouldn't happen if you are the aggressor.

  If you're going to be the boss, use reasonably stout leaders (ten- or twelve-pound is stout enough) and a rod with enough backbone to turn a fish that doesn't want to be turned.

- **Use barbless hooks.** Debarb your hooks by mashing down the barbs with pliers. I take care of this before I even clamp a hook into my fly-tying vise. If you buy your bass bugs, or if someone gives them to you, debarb them right away. It's one of those steps that you're likely to overlook once you're on the water and eager to start casting.

  The best reason for debarbing your hooks is that it enables you to unhook a fish quickly without holding him out of water for a long time or tearing any of his flesh. This will save the lives of fish that get hooked in the throat or gills—which happens quite commonly with bass.

  If you fight a fish properly, you will never lose him because your hooks don't have barbs. In fact, barbless hooks penetrate deeper and more easily and give you a higher percentage of solid hookups than those with barbs.

  Another—not minor—benefit of barbless hooks is that you can back them out of the ear or scalp of your partner or yourself without a trip to the hospital.

- **Deeply hooked fish.** Bass tend to inhale their food. When they hit a moving fly or lure, you'll usually hook them in the lip. But when they take a motionless bug, all too often they get hooked deep in the throat or even in the gills. Setting the hook instantly is not the answer. Usually you'll just pull the bug out of the fish's mouth before he's turned his head and closed his mouth on it.

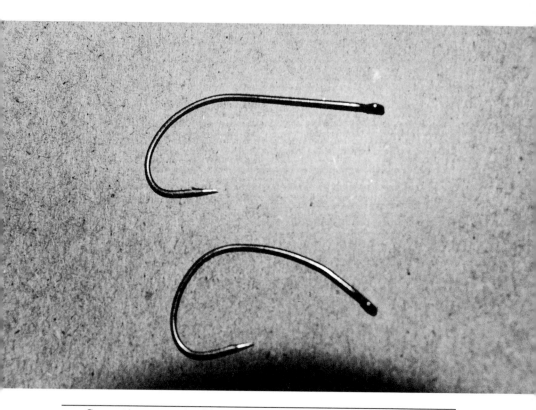

Converting a standard bass-bug hook (top) into a "circle" hook (bottom).

       You can reduce the number of bass you hook deeply by replicating what saltwater fishermen call a "circle hook." With pliers, simply continue the bend of your wide-gaped bass-bug hook so that its point curves upward toward the underside of the shank. Instead of the point being parallel to the shank, as it normally is, you have bent it into an incomplete circle from the beginning of the bend to the point. Now when you tighten your line on a fish, your bug will usually slide out of his throat or gills and catch safely and securely inside his lip. You might save a few bass lives with a circle hook.

- **Land him properly.** A wide, long-handled boat net enables you to land bass quickly and surely, unhook them without excessive handling, and return them safely to the water. Your net should have a small mesh. Wide-meshed nets can catch in a fish's gills and injure or even kill him. There's no need to bring a hooked fish into the boat. Keep the net in the water and simply reach down, and back the (debarbed) hook out.

Because bass do not have teeth, many bug fishermen hand-land their fish and don't bother with a net. Never jam your fingers into a fish's gills, grip him by the eye sockets, or squeeze his belly. When you've beaten the fish, raise your rod to lift his head out of the water and drag him to you. Then clamp his bottom lip between your thumb and the crook of your index finger, which will immobilize him so that you can unhook and release him.

If you're fishing from shore, don't be tempted to drag a bass up onto the bank. This could injure his eyes or gills and will certainly scrape his scales and rub off his protective slime, promoting infection and disease. Land him while he's still in the water, using a net or his convenient lip handle.

- **Don't kiss him.** Fish live underwater. Every second they spend gasping air instead of swimming in the water weakens them and increases their chances of dying. Holding bass out of the water in dry, cold weather will quickly evaporate the natural slime that protects them from bacterial and fungal infections. Handling them excessively under any conditions will destroy their slime.

One well-known television bass wizard likes to lip-grip each caught bass by jamming his knuckles into its throat so that its mouth is forced wide open. He then lifts his trophy high in the air for the camera to admire, bracing its entire weight on his knuckles, and he continues to hold it aloft while he discusses the "bait" he caught it on, the "structure" it came from, the clever strategy he employed for fooling it into striking, the beauty and productiveness of the lake he caught it from, and the terrific meals served in the lodge where he's staying. Then—and I guess he thinks this demonstrates his affection for his quarry—he kisses the poor bass on the nose before tossing it gills-over-tail back into the water.

If he really loved bass, he'd do none of those things.

Fish are designed to swim belly-down in water, not to hang suspended by their mouths tail-down in the air. Lifting a large bass entirely out of the water by his lip can injure his internal organs. If you want to hold him up for a quick photograph, grip his bottom lip with one hand and rest the base of his tail on the back of your other hand. This will minimize his loss of slime.

Lifting a thrashing bass out of the water in a net, dropping him onto the bottom of the boat, or literally throwing him back can injure him in a variety of ways.

The safest way to unhook a bass is to lip-grip him, lift just his head out of the water, and unhook him with your other hand. If he's deeply hooked, or if you've neglected to debarb your hook, reach into his mouth with needle-nose pliers or long forceps. If the hook is so deep that removing it seems likely to injure the fish, clipping the leader and leaving the bug there gives the fish the best chance for survival. Usually the hook will rust, the bug will work loose, and the fish will be none the worse for the experience.

After he's unhooked, use both hands to right the fish in the water. If he seems weak and tired, grip his tail and gently move him back and forth to force water through his gills. Support his belly and keep moving him until you can feel that his strength has returned.

If your bass is bleeding—especially from the gills—when you bring him to the boat, his chances of survival are not good. This is the fish to kill, fillet, bake with bread crumbs, serve with wild rice and a vintage white wine, and eat with ceremonial respect.

The quickest and most humane way to unhook and release a bass.

The Art and Craft
of Bug Making

> "Bass bugs . . . have tremendous appeal for both fish and man. The tying of them seems to bring forth the latent inventive genius of all those who go in for making bugs."
> Joe Brooks, *Bass Bug Fishing* (1947)

> "Whether these lures are made of cork or hair depends, for the most part, on your own preference. Some anglers swear by each type; others swear at them."
> J. Edson Leonard, *Flies* (1950)

> "Bug making has come a long way since the Peckinpaugh cork bug . . . or the clipped deer-hair style that was developed by Dr. James Henshall, probably in the late 1800s."
> C. Boyd Pfeiffer, *Bug Making* (1993)

I have declared my preference for fishing with deerhair over hard-bodied bugs. Deerhair bugs are . . . well, *buggier*—and well-designed ones, at least, are easier than hard-bodied bugs to cast with a fly rod.

But in fact, the objective differences between deerhair and cork, balsa, or other hard-bodied bugs are marginal at best. I've caught most of my bass on deerhair bugs because those are what I usually tie onto my tippet. I suspect that few of those fish would have refused a cork bug, had it been my choice that day.

Undoubtedly my fondness for deerhair bugs comes more than anything from the enjoyment I get from tying them. Spinning and packing deerhair, then sculpting the resulting hairball into something symmetrical and streamlined and elegant, seems to bring out the latent artist who lives in me.

Lashing bird feathers and wild-animal hair onto the shank of a bare hook in a manner that produces something that fish want to eat links me to the first fly fishermen. I like that—which, I guess, makes me a traditionalist.

Many accomplished bug makers find spinning and clipping deerhair fussy, time-consuming, and messy. They prefer carving, sanding, painting, and gluing cork and balsa, and the bugs they create are also elegant and attractive to both fishermen and bass.

Tails, arms, wings, and other bass-bug appendages are pretty much the same on both deerhair and hard-bodied bugs. The difference is the part that makes them float—the body. The bodies of deerhair bugs are made from hollow deerhair, which is tied onto the hook shank one small bunch at a time so that it flares out at right angles and spins 360 degrees around the hook. Each bunch is packed tightly back against the previous one, and when you can't jam any more onto the hook, the whole mess is clipped into shape.

Hard-bodied bugs are made from light, buoyant materials such as cork and balsa, which are carved and sanded into shape and then glued onto the hook.

Making either deerhair or hard-bodied bugs that will take bass requires the right tools, an assortment of materials, and some practice. But in neither case do you need talent. Anybody can do it—and should. Fishing with bugs of your own creation will add a significant dimension to your enjoyment of the sport, guaranteed.

WORKING WITH DEERHAIR

The best hair for bass-bug bodies is the short, stiff, coarse stuff from the back or sides of the deer. Because it's hollow (which, of course, keeps the animal warm in the winter as well as bass bugs afloat), when you bind it tightly to a hook shank, it flares out at right angles. If your deerhair doesn't flare properly, you've probably used hair from the deer's tail or legs, which, unlike body hair, is not hollow.

- **Tools of the trade.** All you need for tying bass bugs are a sturdy vise (to hold the hook while you work), a pair of small, sharp, straight-bladed scissors (to clip and shape the spun deerhair, and to trim away extra materials), and a bobbin (to hold the thread and give you consistent tension while you're tying).

- **Materials.** In addition to several patches of good deerhair in an assortment of colors (for starters, natural white and gray-brown, along with dyed olive, black, green, yellow, and red), you'll enjoy experimenting with materials for wings, arms, and tails. Bucktail (both natural and dyed) makes light tails that tend to float, and makes a bug seem big without adding significant casting weight. Saddle hackle tails, both grizzly and solid, give a bug a lot of lifelike action. Tied back to back so that they splay out, they kick like legs when twitched. Marabou plumes and rabbit strips (again in a variety of colors) pulse and undulate. Tail materials that absorb water and sink will tilt your bug backward, giving it a realistic look in the water. Glittery materials such as Flashabou or Krystal Flash can enhance any tail, although there are times when flash seems to repel rather than attract bass. A few thin strips of rubber for protruding legs, arms, or whiskers do not inhibit casting, and they vibrate seductively even when the bug is resting motionless on the water.

- **Hooks.** Most hook manufacturers now sell hooks designed specifically for bass bugs. They are made of thin wire and have a wide gape relative to their length. Mustad's #37187 and Tiemco's #8089 are well shaped, sharp, and strong.

- **Tying thread.** Working with deerhair requires thread that borders on the unbreakable. Kevlar threads are super-strong, as is Danville's Flymaster Plus. These are what I use for tying bass bugs. Waxing the thread prevents slipping and increases its adherence to the deerhair. The color of tying thread is rarely important, since the fish can see only the tiny "head" behind the hook's eye.

SPINNING DEERHAIR

It takes a little practice to get the hang of spinning deerhair. First, tie in the tail of your bug at the rear of the hook and clip the excess material away, leaving the rest of the shank bare. It's much easier to spin deerhair around a bare hook than one that's layered with thread over the tied-down tail materials. The base of the tail gives you something solid to pack the spun deerhair back against. A drop of glue or head cement over the thread windings where you've tied off the tail will prevent it from slipping and make a smooth-enough base that you can spin deerhair around it, making a good transition from tail to body.

Now, with your thread attached at the base of the tail, you're ready to begin building the body. Between the forefinger and thumb of your left hand (assuming you're a right-handed tier), pinch a small clump from a patch of coarse deerhair and cut it loose. You should now be holding in your left hand a batch of hair about the diameter of a drinking straw. With the forefinger of your right hand, flick the butt ends of the deerhair clump to knock loose the fine underfur, then pick it clean. Some tiers prefer to brush out each clump of deerhair with a toothbrush or mustache comb, which is a bit fussier but does a more thorough job.

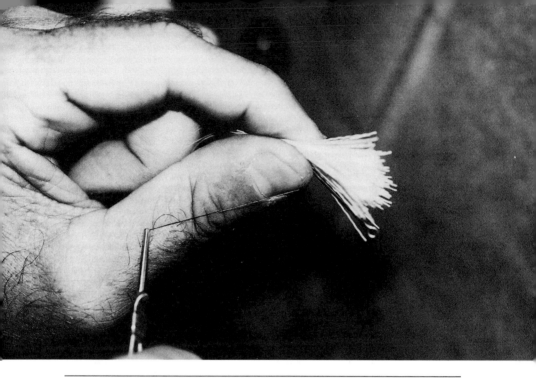

SPINNING DEERHAIR
Pinch the hair against the hook shank.

Make two loose turns around the hook shank and hair.

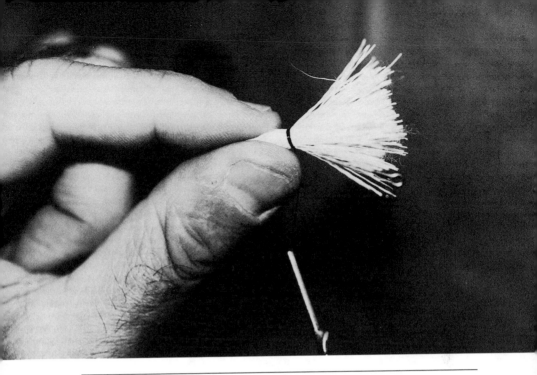

Begin to slowly tighten the thread.

Let go of the deerhair and continue to wind the thread; it will flare and spin.

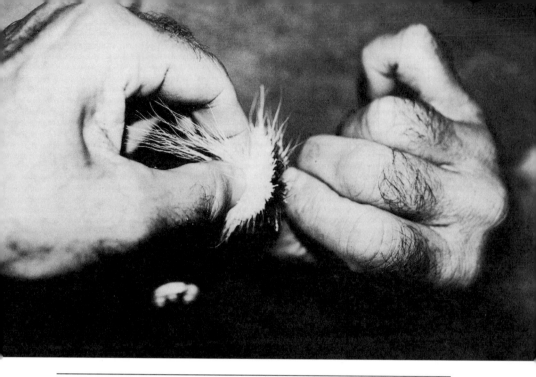

Pack the hair tight between your fingers.

A finished bug before hedge trimming.

Now, still holding the deerhair in your left hand, lay it parallel to or slightly diagonal over the top of the hook shank. With your right hand, make two *loose* thread wraps over the middle of the bunch of hair. Your third turn of thread should be firm, pulling the first two wraps tight in the process. As you make this third turn, let go of the deerhair with your left hand. The deerhair will flare out at right angles to the hook shank and spin around it. Don't stop winding the thread. As the deerhair flares and spins, complete that third wrap and make two or three more tight ones, zigzagging through the flared deerhair. Then pull back the spun deerhair with your left hand and make a couple of tight thread wraps on the hook shank directly in front of the deerhair. Hold the thread tight with a half hitch over the hook between each application of deerhair. Keeping constant pressure on the thread throughout the spinning-and-packing process guarantees a solid finished bug.

Now cut and comb out another bunch of deerhair, lay it over the hook shank in front of the previous one, repeat the wrapping, spinning, and flaring process, and finish with a half hitch.

The secret to a solid, high-floating deerhair bass bug is to pack each bunch of deerhair tightly back against the previous one after you spin it on. So after you've added the second bunch of hair and fixed your thread with a half hitch, pinch the base of the bug's tail firmly between your left thumb and forefinger. Then slide your right thumb and forefinger over the hook shank against the foremost layer of spun deerhair. Push and twist it back against the base made by your left thumb and finger. Don't be gentle with it. The purpose is to pack it as tightly as you can. Some tiers use a packing tool—a thin, hollow cylinder that fits over the eye and shank of the hook—instead of their fingers, but I've found that the twisting motion of my thumb and finger enables me to make denser deerhair bodies than I can with a tool.

Keep repeating the sequence of spinning and packing until the shank of the hook is covered and you cannot possibly add any more deerhair. Make several thread turns in front of the last layer of deerhair behind the eye of the hook, whip-finish, cut off the thread, and add a drop of head cement. Now you're ready to sculpt this shapeless bristle-ball of deerhair into an elegant bass-bug body.

Stacking Deerhair

If you keep your grip on the deerhair when you make it flare with that third tight turn of thread, it will remain where you tied it down rather than spinning around the hook shank. Now you can flare other clumps of different-colored deerhair on each side of it and underneath it.

Stacking rather than spinning deerhair enables you to create multi-colored bugs. By stacking green or olive on top and white or cream on the bottom, for example, you can build a pale-bellied frog-colored bug. With practice, you can even add a few small random stacks of black to the top and sides to represent the frog's spots. Designs like this are very attractive and satisfying to the tier. Whether the fish notice the artistry is another question.

To stack deerhair, first bind down the excess tail material over the entire shank of the hook and cover it with tying thread. This base will help to hold the stacked deerhair in place and prevent it from spinning.

After you've stacked a bundle or two to the top of the hook, remove it from the vise and clamp it back upside-down so you can add deerhair to the underside of the bug. Keep reversing the hook as you work forward, and don't forget to pack it tight with your fingers as you go.

Stack some deerhair over and under the base of the tail even on a bug that you intend to form by spinning. This will cover the thread wraps between the tail and the body, making a smooth transition

---

STACKING DEERHAIR
Lay a new bunch of deerhair over the previous bunch.

The light hair is stacked on the "belly" of the fly, the dark hair on the "back."

and giving the bug a more finished appearance (the bass, of course, couldn't care less).

By stacking two or three clumps of deerhair directly on top of each other, you can create a denser body than you can by spinning.

HEDGE TRIMMING

Whether you've spun or stacked the deerhair, you are now confronted with the lump of clay that needs a sculptor to give it shape. "If you like to trim hedges," wrote H. G. Tapply in *Tackle Tinkering*, "you'll enjoy the next step—barbering the body into the shape you want with scissors."

At this point, your bug could become a flat-faced popper, a bullet-headed slider, a rounded burbler, or a diver. It could be fat or slender, tapered or cylindrical . . . and elegant or ugly. You may see a mouse or a frog or a moth or a baitfish in that dense clump of bristles. What you end up with depends on what you cut off and what you leave.

You can trim the bug while it's clamped in the vise, or you can remove it from the vise and hold it in your hand. Some tiers do their hedge trimming with razor blades or electric barber's razors. I prefer straight-bladed scissors with one-inch blades. Whatever tool you choose, be sure it's sharp.

For almost any design, you should begin by trimming the belly flat and as close as you can get to the hook shank without nicking the thread wraps. For this step, I clamp my bug-to-be upside-down in the vise, which helps me keep the plane of the belly at right angles to the bend of the hook. A flat belly that's curved slightly upward along its outer edges helps the bug float right-side-up and keeps the bite of the hook open to ensure solid hookups with bass.

After you've trimmed the belly flat, remove it from the vise and rough-cut the top and sides into the general shape you want, and then keep clipping and trimming until you've cut away everything except the body shape you visualized. During this process, I hold the bug in my left hand so that I can study its dimensions and symmetry from all angles as I barber it into shape.

FOLDING DEERHAIR
Tie down the tip ends of the deerhair securely before folding. The tail has been wrapped on previously and is hidden underneath the deerhair.

After the body material is wrapped up the shank, fold the deerhair over the back of the fly and tie it down. Trim the deerhair after it has flared.

FOLDING DEERHAIR

By folding the hair around the shank of the hook rather than spinning and clipping it, you can create a smooth, rounded body. This technique is useful for smaller bugs intended to imitate beetles and crickets. Full-sized bass bugs made this way are quite air-resistant and fragile. They neither float nor cast as well as spun-and-clipped bugs of the same size.

To make a folded-hair bug, first tie in whatever sort of tail you want. Then tie in several bunches of long deerhair by their tips at the base of the tail, with the butt ends lying back over the tail, and bind down the tips of the deerhair against the shank of the hook. If you want to add a body to your bug, tie in the material at the rear. Glittery synthetic chenille looks good on this bug. Bring your thread forward to just behind the eye of the hook, wind the chenille forward, and tie it down in front. Now pick up the deerhair, fold it over the top of the shank (being careful to keep it from twisting under the hook), and tie it off behind the eye. The stiff, hollow butt ends will flare. Trim them into whatever shape you want—a small, round head or a wide, flat popper face. At this point, you can tie in wings or legs behind the head if you want. A pair of rubber-leg whiskers sticking out of each side makes an enticing folded-hair bug.

WORKING WITH CLOSED-CELL FOAM

Closed-cell foam comes in five-inch by eight-inch sheets that are one-eighth inch thick. This stuff is composed of tiny self-contained air bubbles. It's lightweight (and therefore easy to cast for its bulk), is easy to work with, compresses nicely under a thread wrap, and is absolutely unsinkable. You can trim foam into shape easily with sharp scissors, and you can tie five or six bass-catching foam bugs in the time it takes to make a single one from deerhair or a hard material such as cork or balsa.

Closed-cell foam bugs don't make the enticing glugs, ploops, and burbles of a deerhair bug, nor do they give you the attention-getting ker-CHUNK of a hard-bodied popper. But because they are so quick and easy to tie, they are relatively dispensable, and I always keep a few in my box for times when I expect (or fear) an encounter with a toothy pickerel or pike. In smaller sizes, foam bugs stand up better than deerhair to an afternoon of bluegill chomping.

You can make a foam Gurgler by following the steps for folding deerhair, substituting foam for the deerhair. First, tie in the bug's tail,

Tying a Foam Gurgler
Tie the foam strip onto the hook.

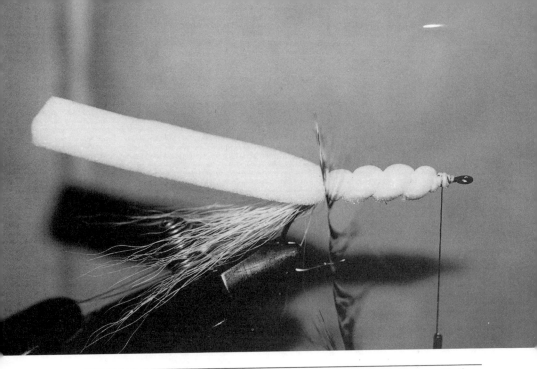

Tie in the hackle. Make widely spaced wraps over the foam with the thread, being careful that the foam strip doesn't twist. Tie off the foam at the head and trim the excess, if there is any.

Wind the hackle feather forward along the path made by the thread. Tie off the hackle and trim.

Pull the foam strip forward and tie off.

Trim the excess foam to create a lip and whip-finish.

lashing all the ingredients to the hook shank and ending with the thread at the base of the tail. Next, cut a strip about half an inch wide and three inches long from a sheet of foam. Lay the foam over the top of the hook shank, with the front of the strip just behind the hook's eye and the rear of the strip extending back over the tail. Tie the foam down at the base of the tail with three or four thread wraps, saturate the hook shank with glue (to prevent the foam from twisting), fold the foam strip around the hook shank, then wind your thread forward over the foam strip, leaving about one-eighth inch between turns, finishing behind the eye. Next, fold the strip of foam that's been extending back over the tail forward over the top of the hook, stretching it tight to form a shellback. Tie it down behind the eye. The remaining front end of the foam will flare slightly upward and over the top of the hook's eye. Trim the excess foam to leave a curved upper lip about three-eighths inch high. This lip will push water and create a burbling commotion and a side-to-side wobbling motion when you retrieve your bug. It helps to stiffen the lip by lightly brushing head cement onto it. To create a slider-type bug, simply cut the foam flush rather than leaving a lip.

To make an even simpler foam bug, first tie in the tail materials plus whatever body, wings, and arms strike your fancy. Then cut and shape a strip of foam, lay it over the back of the bug, and bind it down

---

TYING A FOAM IN-BETWEENER
Tie in the tail and rubber legs.

Tie in the foam strip, then wrap the body toward the eye.

Fold the foam strip forward, wrap once or twice, then fold the strip backward to create a round "head." Wrap once or twice again, trim, and whip-finish.

The finished In-Betweener.

at the base of the tail and at the head. Add head cement to the front and rear winds and it's complete. This bug, which uses less foam than the folded version, floats a bit lower in the water, which actually gives it a little better action when twitched and retrieved.

The shape of a foam bug results from the length and width of the strip of foam you cut. You can make the foam body of your bug short and fat to "imitate" a frog, or long and skinny like a baitfish.

I use white foam for all my foam bugs. Before I tie foam to the hook, I color it with a waterproof pen. Foam takes waterproof colors beautifully. It's a simple matter, for example, to leave the belly white and color the top with a contrasting color—or with several colors. After the bug is tied, you can decorate it with spots and stripes and draw eyes and gills on it if you want. The bass won't object.

WORKING WITH CORK AND BALSA

Bass bugs with bodies made from cork or balsa combine the fly tier's art with the cabinetmaker's craft. The tail portion of the bug is normally tied to the hook just as it is for deerhair bugs. But hard bodies are carved and sanded into shape, slotted, glued to the shank of the hook, and finished with enamel.

- **Tools.** In addition to a fly-tying vise, scissors, and a bobbin, you'll need a sharp cutting tool (an X-Acto knife or a razor), at least three grades of sandpaper, and a hacksaw blade. An electric drill with grinding and sanding attachments makes the job easier. An emery board can also be useful.

- **Cork and balsa.** You can buy these cheap materials in most hobby shops. Look for smooth, unpitted cork. Wine-bottle corks are usable, though they're generally rough and pitted. You can also get both materials already shaped and slotted for bugs from many fly-tying supply houses.

- **Hooks.** Several manufacturers make hooks with kinks in the shank specifically for hard-bodied bugs. The Mustad #33900 and the Tiemco #511S come with a single hump, while the Mustad #33903 is a long-shanked hook with a double hump. The kink in the shank prevents the body from twisting out of line the first time a fish chomps down on it.

- **Glue.** Any strong waterproof glue will do the job. Five-minute epoxy can't be beat.

- **Paints and sealers.** Balsa and cork bodies should be coated with a sealer before they're painted. The sealers, lacquers, acrylics, and enamels available in hobby shops work fine. You'll need brushes of several different sizes, too. Cheap, disposable brushes are my preference, since cleaning them thoroughly enough to reuse is more work than it's worth.

PREPARING THE BODY

Making hard-bodied bugs one at a time is inefficient and time-consuming. Instead, use an assembly-line process. Prepare a dozen or so bodies at the same time. Then prepare the same number of hooks and glue the parts together in a single session. Paint them all at the same time, either before or after joining hook and body.

For a well-balanced and solid-hooking hard-bodied bug, the rear of the body should not extend farther back than the point of the hook. The point should be about midway between the eye of the hook and the tip of the tail.

Solid materials such as cork and balsa can be formed into the same variety of shapes as deerhair. Use a thin knife, a razor blade, or an electric grinder to rough-cut a cylinder of cork or balsa. Then sand it smooth.

Cork and balsa bodies in various stages of preparation.

Next cut a slot for the hook shank. The slot should be deep enough to accept the hook shank, including the hump, but not so deep that the hard body will reduce the "bite" of the hook. Most bug makers prefer sawing the slot with a hacksaw blade rather than making a slice with a razor.

You can seal and paint the body now, or you can do it after you've glued it to the hook.

PREPARING THE HOOK

C. Boyd Pfeiffer, whose *Bug Making* is the bible of the subject, tested several different ways of preparing hook shanks for hard-bodied bugs, seeking the best method to prevent twisting. He discovered that a straight-shanked hook wrapped with coarse thread provided a more solid foundation than a bare kink-shanked hook. Strongest of all was a kinked hook covered with thread and then wrapped with chenille.

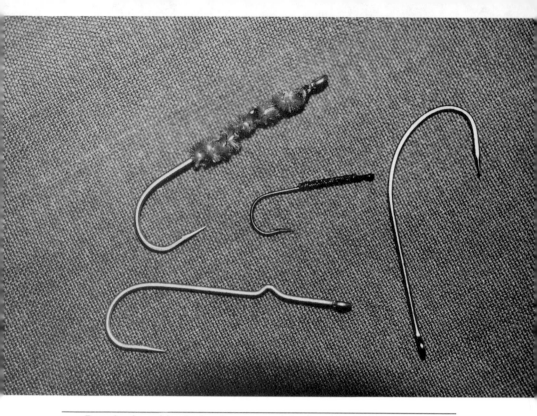

Bare hook and hook shanks prepared for hard-bodied bugs.

Art Scheck, who prefers small (sizes 2 to 8) balsa bugs, uses straight-shanked Aberdeen hooks. "To keep the body from twisting on the hook," he says, "I bind a piece of monofilament along the top of the shank, and then soak the wraps with superglue. That changes the cross section of the hook from round to oval and increases the bonding surface for the glue used to secure the body to the hook. I'm not sure where I learned the trick—probably from Boyd Pfeiffer, the king of piscatorial mechanics."

WINGS AND LEGS

One method of adding wings and legs to the sides of a hard-bodied bug is to cut slots across the bottom of the cork or balsa body, lay in strands of rubber or bunches of bucktail or synthetic hair, and epoxy them in place. You can also drill a narrow hole all the way through the body; poke a darning needle, a bobbin-threading tool, or a piece of stiff wire through the hole; hook some leg material to the end of it; and pull it back through so that the fibers poke out both sides. Add a drop of epoxy to each hole.

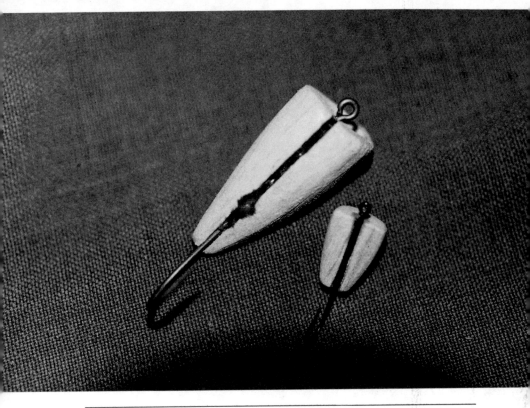

Hook shanks fitted into the cork and balsa bodies.

AN ASSORTMENT OF HARD-BODIED BUGS

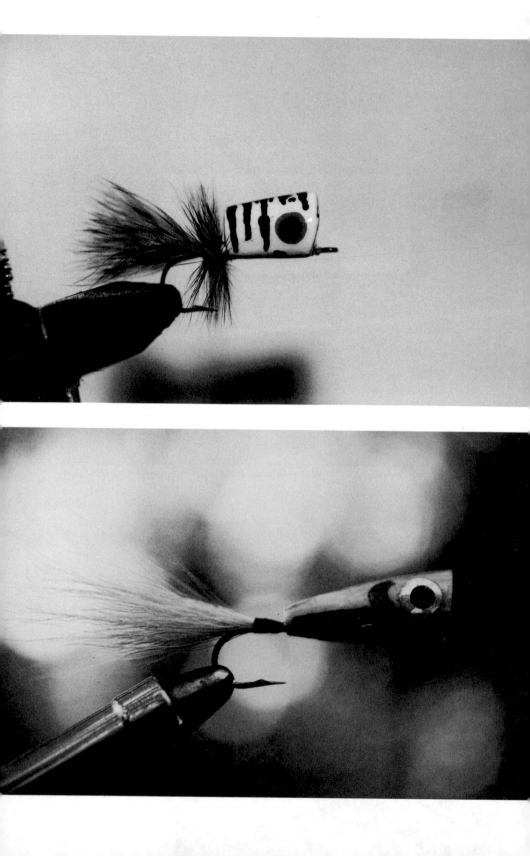

OTHER BODY MATERIALS

In *Bug Making,* Pfeiffer describes how to make floating bugs from such diverse materials as the quills from the wing feathers of turkeys, large-diameter plastic drinking straws, silicone, and a lot of other buoyant stuff. His point is clear: When it comes to making bass bugs, your imagination is your only limitation.

Here are a couple of alternatives to deerhair, foam strips, balsa, and cork that are easy to work with and make effective bugs:

- **Solid foam.** You can buy preformed closed-cell foam bug bodies in a variety of shapes, colors, and sizes from many fly-tying supply houses. These bodies come preslotted or with holes already drilled through their middles to take a long-shanked hook. For bodies with holes, use a straight-shanked hook wrapped with thread. A kinked hook, spiraled with chenille, holds best in a slotted body. Simply tie on a tail, soak the prepared shank with glue, and slide the hook through the hole or wedge it into the slot. When the glue dries, the bug is finished, although you can decorate it with waterproof pens and add eyes if you choose. Foam-bodied bugs cast well and float forever.

- **Synthetic tubing.** Jack Gartside pioneered the use of a nylon-and-polyester tubing called Corsair for an impressive variety of flies, including floaters. Corsair bugs cast easily and land softly, and when sealed (there are several clear, flexible sealers on the market), they float nicely.

    Corsair tubing comes in several diameters. Use the largest (one-half inch) for bugs. Here's how:

1. Tie the tail materials—bucktail, hackle feathers, glitter material, in whatever colors and combinations suit your fancy—onto a thin-wired streamer or bass-bug hook.

2. Wind forward over the tail materials to just behind the eye of the hook.

3. Cut a length of tubing about half an inch longer than the shank of the hook.

4. Slide the end of the tubing over the front of the hook and tie it down behind the eye. Be sure the cotton threads in the tubing line up along each side of the shank. They will serve as lateral lines along the middle of the body.

5. Wind the tying thread back to the base of the tail.

TYING WITH SYNTHETIC TUBING
Tie the tail and tubing onto the hook.

Wrap the thread back and push the tubing back over itself toward the end of the hook.

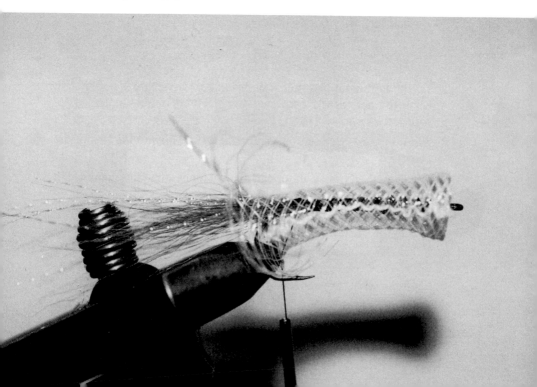

Tie the tubing at the rear of the hook and trim the excess.

Finished bass bug painted and coated with waterproof sealer.

6. Push the tubing back over itself, turning it inside out, so that it encircles the shank of the hook. At this stage, you can form the head into a variety of shapes—cupped, blunt, or pointed—simply by molding it with your fingers.
7. Tie down the tubing at the base of the tail and trim away the excess.
8. Seal the thread windings at the rear with head cement.
9. Decorate the tubing with waterproof pens, darkening the lateral threads with black, and add eyes to satisfy your own artistic urges. Bass will not object.
10. Coat the hollow tube body with flexible, waterproof sealer.

WEEDGUARDS

Bass like to hide in and under brush and weeds, which is where we should cast our bugs if we hope to catch them. Bugs that are designed

A bass bug with deerhair weedguard.

to ride through and over weeds and obstructions without fouling give the fisherman the confidence to cast over the middle of a weed bed or into thick brush. Although you'll usually find fish along the edges of cover, there are times—such as at midday under a bright sun—when bass hang back in it. Under these conditions, especially, the deeper into cover you can cast, the better your chances of catching fish.

The ingenuity of bug designers has produced many different ways of making bass bugs weedless, or nearly so. Boyd Pfeiffer, for example, lists twelve different weedguard designs in *Bug Making*.

Here are three simple ways to increase the weedlessness of deerhair and hard-bodied bugs:

- **Deerhair brush.** When hedge trimming a deerhair bug, leave a "brush" on the belly just in front of the point of the hook. Trim the tips of the deerhair so that they extend just below the point. Stroke some head cement into the brush to add stiffness. For hard-bodied bugs, after you've tied the tail materials onto the hook, turn it upside-down in the vise. Stack one bunch of deerhair at the base of the tail so that it flares around the point of the hook, trim, and stiffen with head cement. Mount the body directly in front of the brush.

  Deerhair weedguards are brittle and not 100 percent weedless, and they sometimes break after a few bass have clomped down on them. But they do slide your bug over and through pretty thick stuff. They add no weight to the bug and they do not seem to reduce its effectiveness in hooking fish.

- **Mono loop.** A single monofilament loop, properly attached to your bug, makes an effective weed-deflecting keel. The mono loop is probably the most widely used weedguard on both deerhair and hard-bodied bass bugs. Here's how to build one into your bug:

1. Before you begin to tie materials onto the hook, lash an eight-inch length of monofilament along the side of the hook shank and bind it down over the beginning of the bend. Add a drop of glue to the wraps. The diameter of the mono depends on the size and weight of the bug. For full-sized bugs (sizes 1/0 and 2/0), thirty-pound mono is about right. For smaller bugs, you can go with somewhat thinner material.

2. Let the mono hang down off the back of the hook while you finish making the bug in the usual way. Trim deerhair bugs. Add the bodies to balsa or cork bugs, and glue and paint them. In both cases, leave about one-eighth inch of bare hook behind the eye.

3. Now bring the mono *through* the bend of the hook (not around the outside of it) to the opposite side, then up to the eye. It should form

a loop that begins inside the bend of the hook, curves down below the point, and finishes at the eye. Run the end of the mono up through the eye, adjust the size of the loop, then tie it down behind the eye. A drop of glue secures it. A mono loop that begins inside the bend of the hook will not twist to the side or flatten the way a loop outside the bend will.

- **Upside-down hooks.** A hook that rides point-up will generally skim over weeds and snags without fouling. Simply tying the fly to the underside of a standard hook, however, does not work. The weight of the hook leads it to land upside-down, and in any case the humped back of the bug seriously compromises its hooking qualities.

  Keel hooks and bend-back hooks are designed to land in the water with the point up. I don't know of any commercial

---

TYING A MONO WEEDGUARD
Attach an eight-inch length of mono to the rear of the hook.

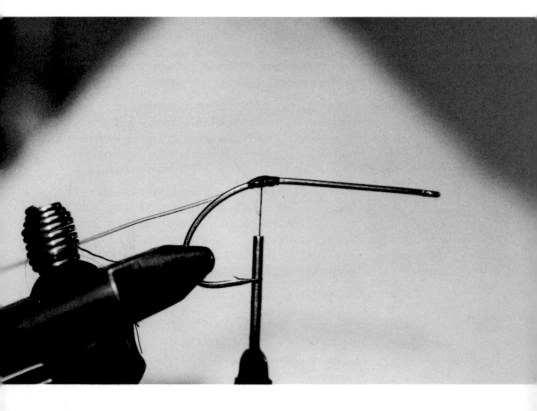

When the rest of the bug is finished, bring the mono up in a loop along the bottom of the bug, and tie it in at the head. Trim the excess.

A finished bass bug with a mono weedguard.

keel or bend-back hooks that are suitable for bass bugs, but you can make your own bend-backs from extra-long standard-wire streamer hooks such as Mustad's #3665A (which is half an inch longer than a standard streamer hook) and #94720 (an 8X-long streamer hook). Grip the hook with two pairs of needle-nose pliers a little to the rear of the center of the shank (depending on the length of the hook) with the bend of the hook down. Carefully bend the forward half of the hook upward to about a thirty-degree angle. Now, when you hold the hook upside-down the way it will ride in the water, the bend of the hook angles downward and curves back up. Insert the hook in your vise with the point up and tie the bug on the straight, forward half of the shank. A long bucktail tail extending over the top of the hook's point increases the bug's weedlessness. Trim the top of the bug fairly flat to maximize the bite of the hook.

Tying Upside-Down Bugs
Hook bent and positioned in the vise.

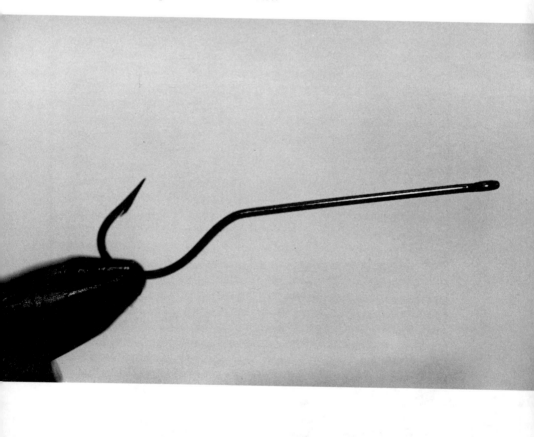

A finished upside-down bug.

8

Designs and Recipes

"I've always wanted to make a bug that was different. Drastically different! I've thought up what it will be. This bug when on the water will look like any other cork-bodied popping bug. But—as you give it a pop— an American flag will spring out of the cork body and wave merrily in the breeze."

Joe Brooks, *Bass Bug Fishing* (1947)

"Bulky bass bugs, with air-catching legs, wings and other projections, do seem more lifelike and provocative to the fisherman, but there is little evidence that bass see them in the same light."

Harold F. Blaisdell, *The Philosophical Fisherman* (1969)

"We have modified many bugs by adding rubber legs and have deliberately hacked up some beautiful creations to make them more attractive. . . . Remember that bass lack artistic tastes."

Charles F. Waterman, *Fly Rodding for Bass* (1989)

When bass-bug fishermen design a bug, their purpose is to catch fish. They try to create a bug that will produce seductive behavior when it's twitched, jerked, and skidded over the water, and they often name their bugs to suggest that behavior—William Jamison's Coaxer, Tom Loving's Gerbubble Bug, Tim England's Tantalizer, Jim Stewart's Lucky Wiggler, Jack Gartside's Gurgler, Larry Dahlberg's Diver.

Bugs that are created with an eye to the commercial market, on the other hand, are usually named after bass prey that they claim to

121

represent—the Cal-Mac Moth, Peckinpaugh's Night Bug, the Wilder-Dilg feathered minnow, Messinger's Hair Frog, Whitlock's Mouserat.

Some bugs, of course, are named whimsically—Tuttle's Devil Bug, Roy Yates's Deacon, the ancient and honorable Sneaky Pete. Tap never did give his bug a name.

Manufacturers believe that fishermen are more likely to buy bugs that they think imitate something, but bass fishermen know that imitating actual prey does not enhance a bug's fish-catching powers. Bass are supremely opportunistic, nonselective feeders. They will eat any bug that acts alive and edible—regardless of what it resembles. Even a cork-bodied bug with an American flag waving atop it would probably look delicious to a bass, provided it blubbed and burbled when twitched.

Besides behaving seductively on the water, good bass bugs are pleasant to cast, durable, unsinkable, and reasonably easy to make.

The shape of a bug's body determines how it behaves on the water's surface. There are four basic bass-bug body types: poppers (which make a loud ker-CHUNK when you give the line a hard tug), chuggers (which gurgle and burble), sliders (which glide and wobble quietly), and divers (which dart beneath the surface when retrieved). Each design is effective, and there are conditions under which one might work better than another.

Tails, arms, legs, and other appendages in different combinations and made from a variety of materials also affect the way a bug acts on the water, and therefore how it appeals to a bass (although it's doubtful that bass translate a bunch of hair or a few feathers as "tail" or "legs"). All of this stuff certainly affects the way a bug appeals to fishermen.

Bass-bug tiers are, inevitably, inventors. Liberated from any need to imitate something, they begin with one of the standard body types (sometimes "improving" it in subtle ways), add appendages, and try different color combinations. They can't help it. Fooling around with shapes, colors, and materials is one of the pleasures of bug making. If the resulting creation catches a bass—which it certainly will if it spends enough time on the water—they proclaim it a success. Sometimes they even name it after themselves. This is entirely harmless.

The fact is, ugly, misshapen bugs catch about as many bass as elegant, symmetrical ones do. But no one wants to buy an ugly bug, and no tier with an ounce of pride wants to make one.

If you're a serious bug fisherman, you'll end up saving money by making your own. Even if you fish for bass only occasionally, you'll find creating and tying your own bugs a rewarding pursuit in its own right. The nice thing about making and fishing with your own bass bugs is that even your earliest, ugliest efforts will catch about as many fish as those of the master tiers if you cast them to the right places.

In a lifetime of spinning deerhair, I don't believe I've produced two identical bugs. I begin with a design in mind (I might want to make a popper or diver, for example), and then I mix and match ingredients, colors, and shapes, as my mood and creative impulses dictate. There is no need to copy any bug pattern mindlessly. I often end up making something quite different from what I had in mind when I first sat down to begin tying.

Let's dispense with the question of color: Use colors that please you, because bass don't much care. As a general rule, dark colors make a sharper silhouette at night and in low light, while light colors are somewhat more visible to bass in daylight. Mix a few strands of Flashabou with each bunch of deerhair that you spin onto the hook, as Will Ryan does, to create a glittery body. Imitate the colors of natural prey if it gives you more confidence. Make your frogs green with cream bellies, for example, and your minnow imitations white and olive with a touch of red at the gills. The bass probably won't care one way or the other. White or yellow on the face makes your bug easier to see, regardless of whatever other colors you use.

The ten bug patterns that follow should be thought of as prototypes rather than inflexible recipes, and I encourage you to experiment and be creative. I've selected these ten from an uncountable number of possibilities because they are all relatively easy to make and require common and inexpensive materials. Except for a couple of foam designs, these are all deerhair creations. If you'd rather carve, sand, and paint cork or balsa, use preformed hard- or soft-foam bodies, or fool around with Corsair than spin, pack, and clip deerhair, simply follow these instructions, substituting those other bodies for the deerhair ones. You'll end up with essentially the same bug.

TAP'S BUG

Ingredients

HOOK: Standard bass-bug hook, such as Tiemco #8089, sizes 4–2/0

THREAD: Kevlar or Danville's Flymaster Plus

TAIL: Stiff, coarse hair from the base of a deer's tail

BODY: Deer body hair, spun and clipped

Tying Steps

1. Wind the thread onto the rear of the hook. Do not cover the entire shank.
2. Tie in a generous sprig of coarse bucktail by its butts at the top of the bend, making a tail about the length of the hook. The butts will flare.

3. Working forward to the eye of the hook, spin and pack deerhair over the bare hook shank until you run out of room.

4. Whip-finish behind the eye, cut off the thread, and add a drop of head cement to the windings.

5. Trim the deerhair on the bug's underside, making a flat belly as close to the shank of the hook as possible.

6. Shape the rest of the spun deerhair. Leave the face of the bug broad and flat, and taper it sharply and symmetrically back to a slender waist at the base of the tail. When you look at the finished bug head-on, it should be a half circle. From the top it looks like an equilateral triangle.

Notes

Tap's all-deerhair bug can be tied in any combination of colors. Natural deerhair works at least as well as anything. White and yellow are good colors for the fisherman's eyes.

As Tap originally designed it, with its large flat face, it's a popper, although it can be made to gurgle and burble depending on how you retrieve it.

ROY YATES'S DEACON

Ingredients

HOOK: Standard streamer hook, such as Mustad #38941, sizes 2 and 4

THREAD: Kevlar or Danville's Flymaster Plus

TAIL: 2 pairs of splayed yellow saddle hackles

BODY: Red, yellow, or chartreuse silk floss

OVERWING: White bucktail

HEAD: Spun-and-clipped deerhair

Tying Steps

1. Start the thread at the bend of the hook.

2. Select four straight yellow saddle hackles of the same size. Line up the tips, marry them into two pairs, and lay them back to back so that each pair curves outward, creating a swallowtail about the length of the hook shank. Do not strip or clip the stems.

3. Tie in the two pairs of saddle hackles at the bend of the hook. Continue pinching them tightly between your left thumb and forefinger as you wind forward over the rear half of the shank. Leaving the fibers on the hackle stems helps secure the tail and prevents it from twisting.

4. Bring the thread back to the base of the tail. Trim away the excess hackle stems and clip off any protruding fibers.

5. Tie in the silk floss at the base of the tail and wind the thread forward to the midpoint of the shank, forming a smooth underbody.

6. Wind the floss forward to the thread, tie it off, and trim.

7. Even up the tips of a sparse (about the diameter of a drinking straw) bunch of fine white bucktail.

8. Tie in the bucktail over the back of the hook. Its tips should extend somewhat behind the bend. Trim away the excess.

9. Spin and pack white deerhair onto the front half of the hook. Be sure to cover the thread winds where you tied down the wing.

10. Tie off behind the eye, whip-finish, and add head cement.

11. Trim the bottom of the deerhair flat.

12. Shape the remaining deerhair into a round head. Leave a few deerhair fibers extending back over the bucktail wing and along the sides.

Notes

The Muddler-like Deacon glugs and burbles when you twitch it and rides low in the water so that all of its parts move. The tail and wing vibrate seductively even at rest. It's exceptionally easy to cast. It's a good idea to impregnate the deerhair head with dry-fly flotant after you tie it. Otherwise it tends to soak up water and sink.

If you want a wounded-minnow imitation, the Deacon is the right shape and rides awash in the surface. The way the flared tails "kick," you can also think of it as a frog.

GERBUBBLE BUG

Ingredients

Hook: Standard bass-bug hook, such as Tiemco #8089, sizes 4–2/0

Thread: Kevlar or Danville's Flymaster Plus

Tail: Bucktail

Body: Spun-and-clipped deerhair

Side whiskers: Saddle hackles

Tying Steps

1. Wind on the thread at the rear of the shank.

2. Tie in a sparse sprig of fine bucktail for a tail.

3. Strip the fibers off one side of a pair of long-fibered saddle hackles. Tie them in by their tips at the base of the tail, one on each side, so that they extend backward and flat, with their stripped sides facing out.

4. Spin and pack the deerhair body, tie off the head, and cut the thread.

5. Trim the top and bottom of the deerhair flat. Taper the sides to the back. From the front, the body should look like a wide rectangle. From the top, it should resemble a triangle with its base at the front and its point cut off at the rear.

6. Clamp the clipped bug into the vise and wind your thread back on behind the eye of the hook.

7. Pull one saddle hackle around the side and forward so that its fibers are pointing outward, parallel to the belly of the bug. Work the stripped stem in deep among the clipped deerhair along the side until it's forced in close to the shank of the hook.

8. Tie the feather behind the eye; trim away the excess.

9. Repeat on the other side with the other stripped saddle hackle.

10. Make a few winds behind the eye, whip-finish, cut off the thread, and add a drop of head cement.

Notes

The flat shape and the side whiskers distinguish the Gerbubble Bug from other deerhair designs. The hackle fiber whiskers vibrate and wiggle wonderfully even when the bug is at rest, while the flattened design reduces air resistance and makes a bug that casts quite well. This bug doesn't make much of a pop, but it glugs and burbles nicely.

Tom Loving's original Gerbubble Bug was made by sandwiching the side whiskers between two thin strips of glued balsa. For a somewhat easier-to-make hard-bodied version, cut slots on each side of a cork or balsa body and glue the hackles into them before mounting the body onto the hook.

As far as I know, Dave Whitlock was the first to tie a deerhair version of the Gerbubble Bug. His way (which I've described here) is considerably less tedious than slotting or sandwiching cork or balsa.

Feathered Minnow

Ingredients

Hook: Standard bass-bug hook, such as Tiemco #8089, sizes 4–2/0

Thread: Kevlar or Danville's Flymaster Plus

Tail: 6 saddle hackles

Skirt: 2 saddle hackles

Body: Spun-and-clipped deerhair

Tying Steps

1. Wind the thread onto the rear of the hook.
2. Marry the six saddle hackles into a pairs, three feathers to each pair. Then match up the two pair so that the concave sides face out and tie them in at the base of the tail. Continue to pinch the hackles against the shank of the hook with your left hand as you make several tight thread winds over the stems. The tail should be half again or even twice as long as the hook.
3. Trim away the hackle stems and the stray fibers.
4. Tie in two webby hackles at the base of the tail.
5. Wind the two hackles together around the thread winds at the rear of the hook, picking out and fluffing the fibers as you wind. The flared hackles should cover the point of the hook. Tie off and trim the excess.
6. Spin and pack deerhair onto the shank of the hook, whip-finish, cut off the thread, and add a drop of head cement.
7. Clip the bottom flat and short.
8. Trim the top and sides of the deerhair into a slender, rounded bullet shape with a pointed nose that widens toward the rear. Take care not to cut away the wound hackles at the rear of the body. On the other hand, this isn't brain surgery, so if you snip a few fibers, no harm is done.

Notes

The Wilder-Dilg feathered minnow was one of the earliest commercial hard-bodied bugs. It remains popular and effective. The long hackle tail undulates in a fishlike manner when you move it through the water, giving this bug the same appeal as a classic feather-wing streamer fly. The hackle skirt prevents the tail from hanging up in the bend of the hook when you cast it and also serves some modest weedguarding duty.

It's a good idea to impregnate the relatively small deerhair head with flotant after you finish tying it. It's not supposed to be a high floater, but it should move through the surface of the water, not under it.

Although this slider-type bug might represent a minnow to the angler, you can also think of it as a snake or worm or giant leech. There's no evidence that it represents anything except an irresistible meal to a bass.

DAHLBERG'S DIVER

Ingredients

HOOK: Standard bass-bug hook, such as Tiemco #8089, sizes 4–2/0

THREAD: Kevlar or Danville's Flymaster Plus

TAIL: Marabou plume

FLASH: 20 or so strips of Flashabou, Krystal Flash, or Glimmer

COLLAR AND BODY: Spun-and-clipped deerhair

Tying Steps

1. Wind on the thread and tie on the marabou tail at the base of the hook. It should be about twice the length of the hook.
2. Tie the flash material all around the marabou so that it extends to or slightly beyond the tip of the tail.
3. Trim away the excess marabou and flash material.
4. Spin and pack deerhair onto the rest of the hook shank.
5. Whip-finish, cut off the thread, and add a drop of head cement.
6. Trim the deerhair belly flat and short.
7. Clip into the unusual diver shape: a pointed nose, a slim tapered head, and a high stiff collar at the back of the head. Leave a few long hairs at the rear flaring back over the tail.
8. Brush a generous coating of head cement on the bottom (only) of the clipped deerhair.

Notes

Larry Dahlberg devised this distinctive shape to make a bug that will dive under the surface when retrieved and drift back to the surface while at rest. Alternating hard yanks with pauses creates an enticing up-and-down swimming motion. The faster you retrieve it, the deeper it will dive. In fact, Dahlberg sometimes casts his diver on a full-sinking line and short leader and fishes it along the bottom, where its bobbing behavior undoubtedly seduces a lot of bass.

Tails can also be made from long rabbit strips, saddle hackle feathers, generous bunches of flashy strips, or combinations of these and other wiggly water-absorbent materials. In all cases, the tail should be quite long relative to the rest of the bug so that it will undulate behind, rather than stick straight up, when you give the bug a yank.

Frog

Ingredients

Hook: Standard bass-bug hook, such as Tiemco #8089, sizes 6–2/0
Thread: Kevlar or Danville's Flymaster Plus
Tail: 4 grizzly saddle hackles, dyed green or olive
Arms: 3 strands of rubber-leg material
Body: Stacked-and-clipped white and green deerhair

Tying Steps

1. Cover the shank of the hook with tying thread, ending at the rear.
2. Marry the saddle hackles into two pairs and tie them on, concave sides facing out. Wind over the stems all the way forward and back, then figure-eight around the base of the tail to flare the hackles widely. Trim the stems and protruding fibers. The legs should be about the length of the hook.
3. Stack the deerhair, alternating green on top and white on the bottom. You'll need to keep reversing the hook in the vise.
4. About two-thirds of the way forward, make a half hitch and rough-trim the deerhair.
5. Tie the three strands of rubber-leg material together with two overhand knots. The knots should be about three inches apart. Do not cut the ends short yet. Figure-eight this three-stranded piece by its middle (halfway between the two knots) onto the hook right in front of the deerhair so that the arms protrude slightly downward and at right angles to the shank. Add a drop of glue to the thread winds to hold the legs in place.

6. Continue stacking the deerhair, ending behind the eye of the hook with a whip finish. Add a drop of head cement.

7. Clip the belly flat.

8. Trim the top into a bulbous, roly-poly frog-body shape.

9. Trim the rubber arms, leaving three short "fingers" protruding past the knots.

Notes

The kicking legs, the rubber arms, the color combination, and the rounded body all give this bug a froggy look. Whether or not bass think "frog" when they see it, they certainly are attracted to the movement of the kicking legs and swimming arms and the blubbing sound it makes on the water.

You can substitute a variety of other materials for the splayed saddle hackle legs. For example:

1. Tie in a bucktail tail such as you would for a Tap's Bug, with white on the bottom and green on top. Then divide it in half, separate the legs with figure-eight winds, and hold them in place with a drop of glue.

2. Stack and trim a small rump of deerhair at the base of the hook first, then tie in the white and green bucktail in front of it. Divide the bucktail and use figure-eight winds to bring the legs down so that they stick out at right angles to the shank. Add glue to hold them. Make thread winds about two-thirds of the way down each leg for knees. Bend the legs outward at the knees and add a drop of glue.

3. You can substitute fine synthetic hair for the bucktail. It's a bit easier to work with, and it sinks better than deerhair, giving the frog a realistic back-tilting attitude while at rest on the water.

4. Bunches of green rubber-leg material knotted at the knees and ankles also make realistic frog legs.

Joe Messinger of Morgantown, West Virginia, invented the ultimate deerhair frog in 1925. His son, Joe Jr., continues the tradition. It's quite a fussy, delicate, and time-consuming job to tie an authentic Messinger Frog (the trick is in the construction of the kicking legs), and if you make a good one, you'll probably think it's too beautiful to waste on an unappreciative bass.

There are, in fact, dozens of frog-imitating bug patterns. There is no evidence whatsoever that bass prefer one over another. The one I've detailed here, which is a simplified version of a Dave Whitlock design, is about the easiest to make.

MOUSE

Ingredients

HOOK: Standard bass-bug hook, such as Tiemco #8089, sizes 6–2/0

THREAD: Kevlar or Danville's Flymaster Plus

TAIL: Thin strip of any limp animal skin. I prefer a black, olive, or brown rabbit strip with the hair plucked off and tapered with scissors to a point. Chamois works well, and a single strand of rubber also looks quite tail-like.

BODY: Natural deerhair, spun, packed, and clipped

WHISKERS: Rubber legs

Tying Steps

1. Tie on the tail at the base of the hook. It should be about twice the length of the hook.
2. Spin and pack the deerhair onto the shank of the hook.
3. Before the last spin of deerhair, tie in a pair of rubber legs for whiskers. Leave them long.
4. Finish packing the hook with deerhair.
5. Clip the belly short and flat.
6. Trim into a mouse shape, with a pointed nose, small triangular head, and a fat, round body. Cut the whiskers to about one inch long.

Notes

I've caught giant brook trout from Canadian rivers by waking deerhair mice across the currents. I do believe those trout mistook my bug for a rodent. I've caught plenty of bass on deerhair mice, too, though I'm less certain what the bass were thinking.

The deerhair mouse is certainly an effective bass bug. It's a chugger that burbles and gurgles when retrieved, and its sinuous tail snaking along behind and its vibrating whiskers in front give it action that bass like, regardless of what you call it.

Bucktail, hackle fibers, and brush bristles also make effective whiskers.

You can make your mouse more realistic by adding eyes (bead-chain painted glossy black and tied in before the last two spins of deer-hair at the nose) and little leather ears, if you like. The bass won't notice, but you will.

DEVIL BUG

Ingredients

HOOK: Standard bass-bug hook, such as Tiemco #8089, sizes 8–2

THREAD: Kevlar or Danville's Flymaster Plus

TAIL: Bucktail

BODY: Mylar chenille, such as Estaz or wound peacock herl (optional)

SHELLBACK: Long, fine deer body hair, folded

Tying Steps

1. Cover the shank with thread, ending at the rear.
2. Tie in a sparse bucktail tail. It should be somewhat shorter than the hook.
3. Even up the tips of a bunch of long, fine deerhair and tie them onto the top of the hook at the base of the tail so that the butt ends extend back over the tail. If the deerhair is too coarse, it will flare too much to work with easily. For larger bugs, you'll need to tie in three or four bunches on top of each other.
4. Wind forward over the tips of the deerhair, then back to the base of the tail.
5. Tie in the Mylar chenille; wind the thread to about one-quarter inch behind the eye of the hook.
6. Wrap the chenille forward and tie off.
7. Pick up the butt ends of the deerhair, fold the whole bunch over the back of the shank, and tie it down behind the eye with several tight thread wraps. Be careful that the deerhair doesn't twist under the hook.

8. The deerhair butts will flare up and over the eye. Trim the flared deerhair into any size and shape you want. You can make a chugger by leaving a small roundish head, or a popper by trimming the deerhair into a broad, flat face.

9. Finish the thread wraps—including those behind the flared head—with head cement. Giving the shellback a light coat of head cement will make it a bit more durable.

Notes

This is a variation of Orley Tuttle's original Devil Bug. Tuttle made his by laying a big glob of deerhair over the top of the hook shank and binding it fore and aft so that both ends flared. The folded-hair method I've described here allows for a longer, more streamlined tail and makes a bug that casts a bit easier than Tuttle's stubby original. It's quite easy to tie in small sizes but becomes increasingly difficult as the hook size gets larger. A big bass-sized Devil Bug is rather air-resistant, too, and a few encounters with a chomping mouth will distort and break the fragile deerhair shellback.

For these reasons, I tie only small ones (sizes 6 and 8 for bass and panfish; 10 and 12 for trout). I've caught a lot of wild brook trout and bluegills and incidental bass on small Devil Bugs, but it's never my first choice for bass.

The Devil Bug is not a particularly good floater. It helps to impregnate the deerhair head and shellback with flotant.

GARTSIDE'S GURGLER

Ingredients

Hook: Standard bass-bug hook, such as Tiemco #8089, sizes 4–2/0

Thread: Kevlar or Danville's Flymaster Plus

Tail: Bucktail

Flash: 6–8 strands of Flashabou, Krystal Flash, or Glimmer

Body, shellback, and lip: Strip of ⅛-inch closed-cell foam

Legs: Grizzly saddle hackle, stripped on one side

Gills: Red saddle hackle

Tying Steps

1. Cover the shank with thread, ending at the rear.
2. Tie in a sparse sprig of bucktail. The tail should be about the length of the hook.
3. Tie in the flash material along the sides of the tail, so that it extends just beyond the tips of the bucktail.
4. Cut a strip of foam about one-half inch by three inches from a sheet.
5. Lay the strip of foam over the top of the hook so that the front of it is just behind the eye and it extends back over the tail. Bind it at the base of the tail with a few tight wraps of thread.
6. Select a wide grizzly saddle hackle, strip the fibers from one side, and tie it in at the base of the tail by its tip.
7. Coat the thread wraps along the shank with glue.
8. Before the glue dries, spiral the thread forward over the foam, binding it to the shank, leaving about one-eighth inch between wraps and ending about a quarter inch behind the eye. Make several tight wraps over the front end of the foam.
9. Wind the grizzly feather forward so that the fibers protrude, following the spiral thread wraps. Tie off and trim.
10. Tie in the red saddle hackle where the grizzly ends and make three turns around the hook. Tie off and trim.
11. Pick up the strip of foam that's been lying over the tail, fold it forward over the back of the hook, pull it tight, and bind it down behind the eye. The remaining foam will flare slightly upward and extend over the eye.
12. Tie off the thread behind the eye under the foam. Whip-finish and add a drop of head cement.
13. Trim the excess foam into a curved lip that's three-eights to one-half inch tall. Coat the lip, including the thread winds where it's tied down on the back, with head cement.

Notes

Boston's Jack Gartside, both famous and notorious as an innovative fly tier, globe-trotting angler, raconteur, and poker shark, has made his Gurgler a staple among East Coast striped bass and bluefish anglers. Jack also catches tarpon and bonefish on Gurgler variations. But he designed it originally for freshwater bass.

The Gurgler is considerably easier and quicker to tie than any deerhair bug, and it casts nicely on lightweight tackle. I prefer the ploop and glug of deerhair bugs, but the Gurgler's foam lip pushes water and makes a satisfactory commotion.

A water-absorbent marabou tail will cause the Gurgler to tip backward when at rest and ride lower in the water, both of which I think enhance its attractiveness to bass.

You can tie Gurglers short and fat or long and skinny depending on how wide you cut the foam strip and where on the hook you tie it down. You get different actions by varying the size and shape of the lip, or you can cut off the lip entirely to make a slider. In small sizes, the Gurgler is a terrific and durable bluegill bug, and on an extra-long hook, it's a mouthful for a pike. A most versatile design.

ART SCHECK'S ALL-SYNTHETIC IN-BETWEENER

Ingredients

HOOK: Aberdeen (or any standard) streamer hook, such as Mustad #3262, sizes 4–8

THREAD: Kevlar or Danville's Flymaster Plus

TAIL: Synthetic hair

FLASH: 6 strands of Krystal Flash

BODY: Estaz

LEGS: 3 rubber strips

SHELLBACK: ⅛-inch closed-cell foam

Tying Steps

1. Cover the shank with thread, ending at the rear.
2. Tie in a sparse tail of fine synthetic hair, such as Ultra Hair or FisHair.
3. Tie the Krystal Flash over the hair.
4. Knot the three strands of rubber around the shank—one at the rear, one in the middle, and one behind the eye. Form the knot on the underside of the shank. Wind forward and back with the thread and figure-eight each rubber strand, adjusting the legs so that they stick out at right angles. Leave them long. Return the thread to the base of the tail.
5. Put a drop of glue at the knot on each rubber strand.
6. Tie in a strand of Estaz at the base of the hook.

7. Cut a strip of closed-cell foam about three-eighths inch wide and about twice as long as the hook. Curve the rear end and lay it over the shank so that the front end extends forward over the eye and the back lies about a quarter inch over the tail. Tie it down at the base of the tail.

8. Bring the thread forward to behind the eye of the hook.

9. Wind the Estaz forward, being careful not to twist the rubber legs out of position, and tie off behind the eye.

10. Tie the forward end of the foam down behind the eye. Roll the protruding strip of foam back on top of itself, tie down to form a bulbous head, and trim. Whip-finish behind the eye (under the foam head), cut the thread, and add a drop of head cement to the head and the thread bindings at the front and back of the foam shellback. Clip the rubber legs an inch to an inch and a half long.

Notes

Art Scheck sent me one of these bugs without comment. It was tied on a size 6 hook, and when I tried it on my local pond, I caught a dozen bluegills, several crappies, and three nice largemouths on it in about an hour. The little bug was obviously versatile and, with its synthetic materials, virtually indestructible. It rode low, and in the water, its big head pushed water, and its tail and legs shimmied deliciously.

Art's concoction is now my choice for fooling around on a summer afternoon when I'm willing to catch anything that is willing to eat. Toward evening I usually switch to a bigger, more serious deerhair bass bug, although I doubt if I'd be seriously handicapped by continuing to cast Art's little foam bug.

Since Art didn't have a name for it, I have taken the liberty of dubbing it the "In-Betweener." I hope he doesn't object.

It can be made in any color combination and in larger bass-bug sizes, of course. The original In-Betweener, the one that Art sent in the mail, was all black.

Books about Bugs

"The shortage of published works on fishing is poor evidence [that fishing wasn't popular in colonial America]; historians, were they so sarcastic, might point out that this is about the same as assuming that because nobody published books about sex in America before the 1800s, nobody was engaging in it. Fishing, like sex, was not a publishable topic."
    Paul Schullery, *American Fly Fishing* (1987)

"Next to the pleasure of reading a favourite fishing book comes that of persuading a friend to read it too."
    Arthur Ransome, *The Fisherman's Library* (1959)

"Fishing textbooks being written by intensely practical men, sometimes omit to remind us, if their authors think of it at all, that fly fishing needs to have a touch of magic about it if we are to enjoy it to the full."
    Conrad Voss Bark, *A Fly on the Water* (1986)

The literature on fly fishing for bass—on bass fishing in general, as a matter of fact—is skimpy and recent compared to everything that's been written about trout and salmon. The first book devoted solely to bass fishing wasn't published until 1881.

As far as I know, just one book focusing exclusively on the subject of bass-bug fishing with the fly rod (before this one) has ever been published, and that was more than half a century ago. Compare that to the hundreds of volumes that have been written about dry-fly fishing for trout over the past three-plus centuries.

Most of the writers who've addressed the subject of bass-bug fishing have done so within a broader context—fly fishing in general, bass fishing in general, or, in several recent cases, fly fishing for bass. Nevertheless, the accumulated bass-bugging wisdom of our century's most respected angling writers is considerable.

I do not pretend that what follows is a definitive, comprehensive, complete, or even representative bibliography on bass-bug tying, fishing, and related subjects. Many of these volumes have been out of print for years and can be purchased only from dealers in old books (although you might find some gathering dust in libraries or attics, and yard sales often turn up treasures). But they all have informed and entertained me both as a fisherman and as the author of the volume you are holding, and I recommend every one of them to you.

Bergman, Ray, *Fishing with Ray Bergman* (Alfred A. Knopf, 1970).

A collection of Bergman's columns from *Outdoor Life*, edited by Ted Janes and published three years after Bergman's death. Although much of the considerable material on bass fishing is outdated, the underlying Bergman wisdom and common sense remain.

_____, *Just Fishing* (Penn Publishing, 1932).

Wisdom and commentary on freshwater fishing, with particular emphasis on trout and bass. Highly anecdotal. Bergman's vast experience and unbounded enthusiasm for fishing shine through every word, and much of his advice remains surprisingly useful after nearly seventy years.

Blades, William F., *Fishing Flies and Fly Tying* (Stackpole and Heck, 1951).

Probably the best—and best-known—fly tier of his time, Blades's patterns are still remarkable for their precise realism. Although he describes how to tie highly imitative frog, mouse, moth, and crayfish flies, the bass bug he named for himself—Blades' Jet—is a nonimitative cork-bodied popper. This book was decades ahead of its time and remains a useful guide for today's precision tier.

Blaisdell, Harold F., *The Philosophical Fisherman* (Houghton Mifflin, 1969).

Anecdotal and, as the title suggests, philosophical essays on fishing for many species by many methods—including bass on the fly rod. Dedicated to "all those sensible people who think fishing is ridiculous."

_____, *Tricks That Take Fish* (Henry Holt and Co., 1954).

For a book that ranges widely over many species of fish and techniques for catching them, the section on bass-bug fishing contains a lot of timeless, down-to-earth wisdom.

Boyle, Robert H., and Dave Whitlock, *The Fly-Tyer's Almanac* (The Lyons Press, 1975).

Well illustrated with clear, step-by-step tying directions, including chapters on Boyle's dragonfly bass bug, Whitlock's deerhair version of the Gerbubble Bug, and Whitlock's Wigglelegs Frog.

Brooks, Joe, *Bass Bug Fishing* (A. S. Barnes, 1947).

Before this one, the only book (which I honor by filching its title) devoted exclusively to surface fishing for bass with the fly rod. There have been many developments in the half century since Brooks's book was published, but his basic understanding and love of bass bugging remain fresh, informative, and entertaining.

Ellis, Jack, *Bassin' with a Fly Rod* (The Lyons Press, 1996).

A comprehensive discussion of tactics and equipment and flies (not limited to bugs—or even to conventional flies), leavened with anecdotes and opinion. Ellis's chapter on the history of fly-rod fishing for bass is especially instructive.

Hauptman, Cliff, *The Fly Fisher's Guide to Warmwater Lakes* (The Lyons Press, 1995).

The most thorough and readable study I know of on the subject of locating bass (and other warmwater species) in lakes and ponds. Especially valuable lore on how weather, water temperature, and season influence the movement and eating habits of bass.

Henshall, J. A., *Book of the Black Bass* (Robert Clarke, 1881).

The first book devoted exclusively to bass fishing. Outdated in many respects, of course, the book nevertheless contains scientific lore and discussions of tactics and bass behavior that make it more than an historical curiosity.

Knight, John Alden, *Black Bass* (G. P. Putnam's Sons, 1949).

The considerable space devoted to tackle, lures, and flies strikes the modern reader as quaint and hopelessly outdated, but the discussions of bass behavior and habits remain valuable.

Leiser, Eric, *The Complete Book of Fly Tying* (Alfred A. Knopf, 1977).

Equally useful for beginners and experienced fly tiers. Clearly written and illustrated, with an excellent chapter on working with deerhair.

Leonard, J. Edson, *Flies* **(A. S. Barnes, 1950; The Lyons Press, 1986).**

After fifty years, still a model of down-to-earth clarity and practical fly-tying advice. The only book I know of with instructions for tying a "strip-skin bob."

Livingston, A. D., *Bass on the Fly* **(Ragged Mountain Press, 1994).**

Comprehensive, often witty, and always highly readable. More emphasis on underwater techniques than on bugging. The section on the mechanics of fly fishing is especially lucid.

Lyons, Nick, "The Bass Fly Revolution" (*Field & Stream*, **May 1990).**

A celebration of the revolutionary bass designs of Dave Whitlock, both surface and subsurface, and the joys of fly-rod bass fishing.

_____ (ed.), *The Quotable Fisherman* **(The Lyons Press, 1998).**

An endless source of entertainment and amusement for all anglers.

McClane, A. J., *The Practical Fly Fisherman* **(The Lyons Press, 1989).**

Originally published in 1953 and not revised for this reprint; the chapter on bass is a bit dated. McClane's discussion of the history of bass bugs reflects his encyclopedic knowledge of all things angling.

_____ (ed.), *McClane's New Standard Fishing Encyclopedia* **(Holt, Rinehart & Winston, 1965).**

Brief but authoritative entries on everything related to fishing—species, lures and flies, tackle, destinations, and history.

Murray, Harry, *Fly Fishing for Smallmouth Bass* **(The Lyons Press, 1989).**

Murray is probably our foremost authority on catching smallmouths from rivers on flies, and this book emphasizes moving-water techniques and situations, the imitation of bass prey, and subsurface flies.

Nixon, Tom, *Fly Tying and Fly Fishing for Bass and Panfish* **(A. S. Barnes, 1968).**

At its time, this was the definitive and most encyclopedic book on the subject. By the creator of the marvelous Calcasieu Pig Boat—a sort of underwater bass bug.

Ovington, Ray, *Tactics on Bass* (Scribner's, 1983).

Dissects every imaginable type of bass cover in lakes, reservoirs, and rivers, and describes how to fish each of them effectively, with abundant charts and diagrams. Not specifically a fly-fishing book, but informative for all serious bass fishermen.

Pfeiffer, C. Boyd, *Bug Making* (The Lyons Press, 1993).

The one indispensable book on making bass bugs from every imaginable material and by every conceivable method.

Ryan, Will, *Smallmouth Strategies for the Fly Rod* (The Lyons Press, 1996).

Simply the best book on the subject—comprehensive, opinionated, witty, up to date, and delightfully anecdotal.

Schullery, Paul, *American Fly Fishing* (The Lyons Press, 1987).

The definitive history, beautifully written and thoroughly researched by the former executive director of the American Museum of Fly Fishing.

Sosin, Mark, and Lefty Kreh, *Practical Fishing Knots* (The Lyons Press, 1991).

The indispensable book on knots of every imaginable use for fishermen. Well illustrated with crystal-clear directions, plus discussions on the strengths, uses, and limitations of each knot.

Stewart, Dick, *Bass Flies* (Northland Press, 1989).

An excellent handbook for the tier of all kinds of bass flies. Larry Largay's illustrations of tying steps and flies are superior, and Stewart's directions are crystal clear. The sections on spinning and stacking deerhair could not be improved.

Stewart, Dick, and Farrow Allen, *Flies for Bass and Panfish* (Mountain Pond Publishing, 1992).

Color photographs with concise tying directions for dozens of bass bugs, as well as scores of other flies for bass and panfish.

Sturgis, William Bayard, *Fly-Tying* (Scribner's, 1940).

Surprisingly up to date after more than half a century, this book emphasizes the "principles of construction," offering the Henshall Bug as the model for spun-deerhair bass bugs and the "cork head minnow" for making cork bugs.

Tapply, H. G., *The Fly Tyer's Handbook* (Oliver Durrell, 1949).

Out of print and hard to find. My father's chapter on spinning and trimming deerhair is still, after fifty years, the most concise and lucid I've read.

_____, *The Sportsman's Notebook* (Holt, Rinehart & Winston, 1964).

The best stuff from thirty-five years of columns in *Field & Stream.* Ranges broadly over hunting, fishing, camping, and other outdoor topics, with several commonsense entries on bass fishing with the fly rod and bass-bug design, along with many of Tap's famous tips.

_____, *Tackle Tinkering* (A. S. Barnes, 1946).

Also a collectible. Some outdated material on the care and repair of tackle, but the chapter on fly tying includes clear, straightforward, and ever-useful instructions on making both cork-bodied and deerhair bass bugs.

Warmwater Fly Fishing (Abenaki Publishers, Inc.).

This bimonthly is, as far as I know, the only magazine devoted exclusively to fly fishing for warmwater species, with particular emphasis on bass. Articles by well-known fly-fishing writers explore destinations, tackle, methods, and fly designs. C. Boyd Pfeiffer's regular column, "Boyd's Bughouse," is always of particular interest.

Waterman, Charles F., *Fly Rodding for Bass* (The Lyons Press, 1989).

After more than half a century, Charley Waterman is still one of our best outdoor writers—always conversational, entertaining, and informative. This slender (eighty-nine pages) volume is full of common sense on tackle, techniques, and bass flies, including bugs.

Whitlock, Dave, *L. L. Bean Fly Fishing for Bass Handbook* (The Lyons Press, 1988).

The most comprehensive and clearly written book of its kind for beginners by our most influential fly-rod bass fisherman and the creator of dozens of innovative bass flies.